INNOVATE WITH INFLUENCE

Tales of a High-Tech Intrapreneur

By

Steve Todd

GOOD LUCK JONAS,

STEVE

BookLocker.com, Inc.
2009

To my co-workers past and present

Acknowledgements

Special thanks to Chuck Veit and Nancy Rosenbaum

for their help with graphics and editing

Table of Contents

List of Figures

INTRODUCTION

I kicked up my feet onto my desk, leaned back in my chair, and listened to my company's internal talk radio show. My laptop was open, and images of the talk show guests danced across the screen.

Today's topic was personal branding. One of the guests, Dan Schawbel, was making the argument that employees throughout the company should be aware of (and develop) their own personal brand. A personal brand is an important aspect of an individual's career development. The ubiquity of the Internet makes it easy for prospective employers to learn about a candidate with just a few well-placed keystrokes. What information is out there? Are there ways to control what is discovered? What does your own personal brand look like?

Dan and I had discussed this topic on several occasions, and I have to admit to a fairly high degree of skepticism. I'm in my forties, Dan is in his twenties. People of my generation perceive the concept of personal branding as self-promotional, something to be avoided at all costs. Dan countered my protests with what I had to concede might be a valid statement: People who control their personal brand have an edge in the job market.

The radio banter shifted to the intersection of personal brand with employer brand. I leaned in a little bit closer. I hadn't considered this angle.

If an employee has a personal brand (whether it's a good one or a bad one), the employer's brand can be affected (either positively or negatively).

As listeners began to ask their questions, I found myself agreeing with the overall statement. And I started asking myself a few questions.

"What's my personal brand?"

"Would the development of my own personal brand help my company?"

It would never have occurred to me to control my personal brand, but even the most old-school employee will consider an opportunity to help his or her company, especially since doing so also helps the employee.

As the host signed off the air, I kept the conversation alive in my own head. I'm a software engineer. I build products. Customers buy them, and then I build more products. How can I make a brand out of that? I would need to do better. I asked myself a different question.

"What would differentiate me from others when looking for a job? How would I sell myself?"

Everyone should be able to answer that question for themselves. I realized my own answer was a simple one.

I'm an inventor. I've come up with dozens of ideas. But that's only half of my story.

The other half is that I know how to build and deliver those ideas.

I'm an intrapreneur (a corporate version of an entrepreneur). An intrapreneur innovates and delivers within a large corporation. That's my brand. I've often thought that I could write a book on my experiences as an intrapreneur. After listening to the radio show, I decided that maybe I should do just that. After all, it would help my company.

But who would read it? Should I just write it for fun, or write it to be read?

I spent some time over the next few weeks outlining a chapter, rearranging ideas and concepts and angles and approaches. After thrashing around for several days, I understood I had a lot to say, but I didn't know who to say it to!

And then it hit me. My career in innovation started immediately upon college graduation, and it's been on a roll ever since. I imagine there are a good many college students looking to make an immediate innovative impact in their field and might need some idea about how to go about making it happen. I started writing this book for them. It doesn't matter, really, whether these students are software engineers. My experience, I reasoned, is applicable to any student, no matter what major.

Then it dawned on me that another potential audience is perhaps just as large and even more interested in how my particular approach to innovation might be applied. Over the years, I have encountered hundreds of employees in many different industries who were less than satisfied with their innovative output. They feel that their ideas are often ignored, and their desire to make a difference is replaced by disillusionment. I realized that many of them could benefit from one simple piece of advice: build your influence first. So I began to write for them as well.

Yet another angle emerged. What about the managers of innovative employees? How can they enable innovation within their organizations? Do they recognize their employees' talents and do they know how and when to get out of the way? Should managers innovate? I added managers as an important aspect of the book.

And what about corporate executives? Many of them will claim that they want their companies to be innovative. How do they encourage innovation? How do they locate their innovators? What do they do once they find them? Which corporate processes and programs are detrimental to innovators, and which are empowering? Innovation perspectives for corporate executives were added to the book.

I also surveyed the landscape of books about innovation. Many of the more recent books on innovation were written by researchers and consultants. These books are loaded with data related to innovation. In-depth studies of multiple corporations are summarized, and conclusions are drawn. If you want data and conclusions, those books are probably fine. If you want stories about personal innovation, those books would leave you hungry. This book is my personal innovation story. It describes a success formula that isn't taught in colleges, corporations, or management books. How does personal innovation, within a corporation, really work? The answer to this question can be immediately deployed for both personal and corporate success.

I had one additional and very tangential audience in mind when I started writing this book. Throughout my career, I have built the products that take care of the world's information. I wondered if people really knew where their information went when a bill was paid online. This book, at least in part, answers that question. The flow of information, from consumer to disk drive, is not generally understood and it's not as mysterious as some might imagine it to be. The technology behind the world's information is described at a very high level. I don't expect you to be able to build your own array in the back yard or write your own software to operate it. The intent of this book is to generate ideas and illuminate the path to help those ideas mature into products.

Customers that purchase high-tech products understand the plumbing behind the flow of information. What they perhaps don't know is the thought process of the people who

4

create and build these products. This book gives them an inside look.

I'm fortunate to have the job that I do. I thank my lucky stars and my high school guidance counselor who nudged me into this industry. Along the way to this point in my career, I've discovered that employees in the high-tech information industry play a grand role in the history of humanity. We build the technology that houses and protects the world's information. The population at large expects their information to always be at their fingertips, safe and secure. They're really not interested in the low-level plumbing; they just want their information.

It's up to the builders of those technologies to make sure that happens. But "builder" is not the word that I prefer to use.

I prefer the word *caretaker*.

SECTION I: INFLUENCE

1. A Day in the Life of a Caretaker

I am a caretaker of the world's information. I also use this term to describe my co-workers. I've been doing this job for over twenty years, but I still couldn't do it in my sleep.

I am one of those folks who awakens instantly. When my eyes pop open at 5:15 a.m. each morning, the gears of my brain engage immediately and my thought processes are launched. I automatically sequence the expected tasks and problems I will encounter in my role as an information caretaker.

What if the disk storing the information fails?

What if a temporary power outage occurs in the midst of an information transfer?

What happens if the information becomes corrupted?

Is the information tamper-proof? If not, where in the process is it susceptible to tampering, by what means, and by whom?

Clearly, there are always problems to be solved. Apparently, my subconscious is always raring to go, urging me to spend every spare moment solving them. Time that could be spent sweeping the night's cobwebs from the corners of my brain is time that would be wasted.

I don't necessarily like waking up this way. I'll stir around in the bed a little bit, trying to shake off these thoughts and delay the day for a few minutes. This movement inevitably causes my dog to stick his cold, wet nose in my face. Dogs don't care about the world's information and its integrity. They care about going out and eating breakfast on schedule. If it's 5:15 a.m., it's time to go out and then have breakfast. Somewhat reluctantly, I push back the covers, bumble down the stairs, and let him out to take care of a dog's business in the backyard. The dog, the kids, my wife, and the daily trip to the local YMCA occupy my primary thoughts until just about 8:30 a.m., at which point I leave the Y and drive to work. My secondary thoughts are on caretaking.

I usually begin my official workday at the office by getting up to speed on what's going on in the information industry; this activity consumes the first ten minutes of my time in the office. Near my desk I keep a piece of paper that reminds me of what I need to do each day. The first portion of the paper lists my quarterly goals. The rest of the paper is fun stuff. Actually, there's a good chance that what's on the rest of the paper includes the next new thing in information caretaking. Even though I might want to dive right in and start working on the fun stuff at the beginning of the day, I work on my goals instead. For my entire career I have had the exact same goal: build outstanding software for the information industry.

I work on my goals every day. I don't mean I work "on" the goals, fine-tuning and changing them; I work on achieving them. My goals might include reading about how the world (more precisely, a customer) wants the next product to work. It might include writing a description of how to build software, or how to test software. It might include writing the software itself.

In the beginning of my career, I slaved like a cave troll, typing on my keyboard in the secluded semi-darkness of my windowless cubicle. I had always had an anonymous existence in my role as a caretaker, and I was okay with that. My own family didn't know the extent of my role as an information caretaker and, for the most part, neither did the majority of the people at my company, including my superiors. I used to spend hours working alone. Actually, I used to spend years working alone.

Not anymore.

Influence: A Day in the Life of a Caretaker

The job of taking care of the world's information has achieved a much higher profile in recent years. I am no longer anonymous. This is a problem.

Anonymity allowed me to innovate and deliver. Over the years, I created and delivered dozens of products that take care of the world's information.

This is why I use the word caretaker to describe myself and my co-workers. We're not personally taking care of the world's information; it's the software we helped create that does the real work. Roughly one million copies of "our" various software packages are running at locations around the world, silently storing and protecting the world's information.

Employees at companies around the world, not just the one I work for but competitors new and old, are trying, just as we are, to build the next new thing. New products are always being developed to create, send, capture, sort, store, duplicate, secure, protect, retain, search, destroy, and retrieve information. In the scramble to capture information technology market share—or just about any other industry market share—I often read that the most innovative companies will win.

The trouble with that statement is that companies aren't innovative; employees are. Stories about employee innovation are among the most interesting reads in the high-tech market. My former company had a Pulitzer prize-winning book written about employee innovation: *The Soul of A New Machine*.

This book contains my personal story. I didn't start out to be a caretaker. In fact, as I was approaching graduation day at North Andover High School in 1983, I didn't know what I wanted to be. I had only applied to one college: Plymouth State College in New Hampshire. My guidance counselor asked me why. Rather than make up some clever excuse, I responded with the unvarnished truth.

Influence: A Day in the Life of a Caretaker

"Because I like to go camping," I told her. She rolled her eyes.

I went camping every summer in New Hampshire. It was awesome.

"Steve," she replied, somewhat exasperated, "your SAT scores are off the charts! Apply to some other schools as well! What kind of career do you want, anyway?"

I shrugged.

"If you don't know what you might like to do, why not think about something in computer science. You did well in that course, and software engineering is a hot field right now."

I took her advice. I applied to several other colleges and specifically those with computer science programs. Several of them accepted me, but I only had eyes for one.

In September 1983, I began my freshman year at the University of New Hampshire. I learned how to write software and, in June 1986, I started a co-op job for a computer company located just off-campus: Data General. I joined as a software engineer in the disk storage division. At that time, Data General employed just over 18,000 employees.

The pay was great. I was making more than $10 an hour and could work whenever and however much I wanted. The job itself was fascinating and, after a few months, I approached my boss about securing a full-time position after graduation.

I was hired as a full-time employee in 1987, right out of college. Within months, I was given an assignment that changed not only my career, but also influenced the path of the storage industry.

My boss handed me a research paper written by someone from the University of California at Berkeley and said, "Read this and start thinking about how you'd build the software to implement it."

Influence: A Day in the Life of a Caretaker

So I did. The paper described a technique, just a theory, really, that would be useful in building a fast, reliable, and cost-effective disk storage system. The theory was called the redundant array of independent (or inexpensive) disks (RAID). The software to implement the theory, setting fire to this new technology, would be called FLARE®. FLARE was my first big job.

Twenty-two years later, hundreds of thousands of copies of FLARE are running on RAIDs installed around the world, providing fast and reliable storage to millions of users and thousands of businesses.

I'm still writing software for the information industry, except now I work for a company called EMC. As of 2009, EMC employs well over 35,000 employees. What happened to Data General, my first employer? They're part of EMC.

During those twenty-three years of software development, I've participated in the generation of over one hundred and fifty patent applications. Many people don't believe that patents are a good or valid measure of innovation. I disagree with those people. When you strip the legalese from those patent applications, three things stand out:

1. A description of a customer problem.
2. A unique and novel solution to the problem.
3. A thorough description of how to effectively build that solution for the customers having that problem.

Are these three items not the essence of innovation? You bet they are! Well-written patents are definitely a measure of innovation.

During my career I've worked with no less than ten different software teams. Each team delivered a product that was shipped to paying customers, and most of these products are still being shipped in some form or other. To date these products have generated a sum total of nearly $10 billion in revenue for EMC.

All of these products started with innovation. The revenue that these products have generated—mind you, this is just the one's I've worked on—is a testament to the power of personal influence.

I've consistently collaborated with others to take new ideas and realize them. Looking back, it's easy for me to see the pattern, a repeatable combination of innovation and influence. I've continually generated innovative solutions to customer problems—even problems they didn't yet know they had—by using what I now call Venn diagram innovation. This is not to say that using this technique to innovate is enough to achieve actual innovative success (especially at a large company). In order to consistently deliver innovation, I had to develop influence first. Influence is based on reputation.

That's what this book is about. There is a method for building influence that is unique to innovators. This method often goes against the grain of conventional thinking. It requires choices in the areas of visibility, career paths, and horizon scanning. I've executed these techniques dozens of times and the results speak for themselves. Although I'm still "just a software engineer," I've joined with my co-workers to create a deep and long-lasting innovative impact on not only our company, but on the industry as well.

I do not believe the popular misconception that good ideas typically become lost at large companies. In fact, innovation at a large company should actually be easier (this also goes against the grain of conventional thinking). I do believe, however, that good ideas will get lost if they are proffered by a person who is not influential.

Influence: A Day in the Life of a Caretaker

Developing influence must trump practicing innovation in the greater scheme of career success. Influence must come first. For this reason, I present my story in two different sections. This first section highlights how I built my influence and maintained it throughout my career. I did not become a one-trick pony; whenever an idea hit the big time, I started anew to find the next big idea.

The second section highlights a personal innovation process I used within a large corporation (EMC). The influence I established, when combined with the disciplined innovation techniques that I used, had a direct and very positive impact on EMC's bottom line. I accomplished all of this while maintaining relative anonymity. When EMC eventually took steps to establish an advanced culture of innovation, they found me.

When I started my career, I didn't have any ideas. It didn't matter. Ideas were given to me, and I used them to build my influence first.

2. Getting it Done

In the first nine months of my career, very little of what I did could have been called "innovation." Was I creative? Sure. But I didn't focus on innovation in the first few critical months of my job. Instead, I focused on one very simple concept: Getting it (whatever "it" was) done.

I built my influence carefully, by becoming known as a person who gets it done. In this context, "done" is meant to imply that all of my assignments were finished with quality. If I approached a deadline with software that I characterized as poor quality, then I was not done. I wasn't prepared to say it was done, whatever it was, until it was done well and properly.

I knew instinctively that there was only one thing better than getting it done, and that was getting it done early. Getting it done early yielded two positive benefits. First, it cemented my reputation as a hard-working, trustworthy, reliable, and productive employee. Second, it resulted in freedom for both my manager and me. My manager had the freedom to give me the big, challenging jobs, and I had the freedom to choose the work I found most attractive. When my company was ready to launch an interesting new project, I had already proven I could get it done, whatever it was, and I often was given the new work.

I definitely got it done during my first few months as a full-time employee working on the FLARE software. My performance during that period had a significant and positive impact on my career in many unexpected ways.

In October 1988, I was given the task of implementing RAID technology in six months. For those unfamiliar with the technology, I offer this simplistic explanation. RAID technology spreads data across multiple disks (for speed), while spreading *parity* information across those same disks (in case one of the disks fails). Parity can be defined as internally generated data that allows for information reconstruction after a failure. The FLARE software I was developing, when built properly, would accept a request to write new information, generate the parity for that information, and then spread all of the information across a set of disks. The software would also accept a request to read the information that had been written to the disks, locate the information on the disks, and return the correct information, even if one of the disks had failed. This feat had never been tried before.

Here's where the principle of getting it done came to the forefront. My deadline was six months away, in April 1989. I decided, even before I started, that I was going to beat that deadline. I made a promise to myself that I was going to walk up to my boss in March and say, with complete confidence, "It's done". I also decided that nobody would be able to break my software during testing. Not only was it going to be done early, but it was also going to be software of the highest quality.

There's one other goal I set for myself. I decided I was going to work diligently for eight hours, and only eight hours, a day. I also vowed that, three times per week, I would drive the one mile from my office at Data General to the campus of the University of New Hampshire and play pick-up basketball. I would not turn in my work early at the cost of being a burned-out wreck. I intended to turn in my work early and be fresh for the next task. I made an effort to leave the workplace each day and rid my mind of RAID technology until I returned to the office the next workday.

These were lofty goals and they were made when I was a relative kid. Were they naïve? I didn't think so at the time, and I still don't. I was fresh out of college and, thanks to my high school guidance counselor's suggestion to pursue some career in computer science at a well-respected university; I had received proper training in formal software design techniques. These techniques emphasized, among other things, the importance of flowcharts, pseudo-code (a textual description of about-to-be-written software code), the appropriate ratio of time spent on design versus coding, and the value of reducing complexity by using state machine techniques. The techniques provided structure and discipline to guide the software development process. The pseudo-code is not elegant, but it allows the reviewer to visualize the intended sequence of actions, checks, and possible gaps.

I didn't forget what I had been taught. I had been trained in the best practices in my field of expertise, and I put them into practice. I didn't take shortcuts then and I don't take them now. There wasn't a lot of glory in the execution, but I got it done the right way. The right way was not only the key to quality software, but it was the key to getting it done early.

My boss asked me to write a piece of software known as the message dispatcher (MD). The MD would be part of the larger FLARE software architecture. The MD software would execute the RAID algorithms on behalf of every disk in the system. I wasn't the one who came up with the idea for the RAID algorithms. I wasn't the one who came up with the larger FLARE software architecture. I wasn't the one that came up with the six-month estimate. Until I was handed the actual assignment, I had made zero intellectual contributions to the end product. In October 1988, I had simply been asked to do a job.

I accepted the task and, upon leaving my manager's office, headed directly to the supply cabinet on my floor and pulled out some pencils, a plastic drawing template for mechanical engineers, and some sheets of 11" X 17" paper. At the very top of the paper, I drew a circle, and labeled it "State

1." Then I created a software design document on my desktop and started a section called "State 1." In this section, I wrote pseudo-code that roughly looked like this:

```
Receive a request to write data

If my disk is healthy

     Proceed to State 2

If my disk has failed

     Proceed to State 3

If my disk is rebuilding

     Proceed to State 4
```

When I had finished this piece of pseudo-code, I had some questions to answer: What did the request to write data look like? I created a new section in my design specification and called it "Data Structures." In this section, I wrote more pseudo-code that looked more or less like this:

```
Message Dispatcher Request Block
{
        Sender
        Size
        Disk Offset
        Peers
        Data
}
```

Then I returned my attention to my diagram and drew three more circles. I labeled them "State2," "State3," and

"State4." I drew an arrow from State1 to State2 and labeled it "Disk Healthy." I drew an arrow from State1 to State3 and labeled it "Disk Dead." I drew an arrow from State1 to State4 and labeled it "Disk Rebuilding." Then I returned to my specification to write the pseudo-code for the three new states. I repeated this sequence — the pondering of possibilities, the identification of options, the drawing and labeling of pathways, and the documenting of the intended design — time and time again.

I did this activity for the entire month of November. I did it for the entire month of December. When January 31, 1989, rolled around, I was still designing the RAID algorithms. I hadn't written one line of actual software. The number of states grew, and each state had a set of success or failure permutations that had to be managed appropriately. What happened if a disk returned an error in the middle of a write/read operation? What happened if the disk simply disappeared? What happened if two requests tried to write data to the exact same location at the exact same time?

The worst possible error a data storage system can make is to return the wrong data and tell the customer the data is correct. If a customer asks for his bank balance, the system must retrieve and deliver the correct answer. With RAID technology, a new situation was occurring for the very first time in the industry. If a customer asked for data from a disk, and that disk was gone, this meant there was no physical copy of that data to be found anywhere in the system. There was no "mirror copy." My software had to re-create the data using mathematical techniques. This was the intended purpose of the MD software. The MD software had to be airtight, or it could very easily return the wrong data to the customer. Customers have every right to demand data integrity from their storage systems; their businesses and their clients depend on it.

For three solid months, I planned the software I was about to write. I became the leading expert, not just in my company but in the entire world, for my implementation of RAID. I left no possible path unexplored. Was my boss a little bit nervous that it was February and I hadn't written a line of software? You bet. Was I nervous? Not in the least. My pseudo-code was made up of very short sentences. It was all-encompassing and comprehensive. The software would be easy to write, once I had completed the design and received approval of the design.

At the beginning of February 1989, I held a design review of my software. This design review occurred in front of some of the brightest and most experienced storage engineers in my company. As I walked these engineers through my software design, I fielded a lot of tough questions. I learned some things I hadn't known and I think I surprised at least a few of them with a number of things they hadn't known. The end result was that nobody could fault my design. After spending three months wrestling with an amorphous problem, I was the expert.

That day was the first day my influence grew beyond my team. Nobody thought I was innovative. I had used the same standard software design techniques used by everybody else in the industry. The difference was that I had worked with undivided attention to detail and I had worked fast.

I started writing my software at the beginning of February. At the end of February, I was done. We didn't have any hardware on which to test the software, but we had a simulator that allowed me to fully test my algorithms in a software-only environment. It wasn't the real thing, but it worked. I walked up to my boss and said, "I'm done."

I was two months early.

Needless to say, my boss was pleased. He had a larger schedule for the entire project, and now he had a free set of hands to tackle other items on the to-do list.

I didn't need any time off before starting my next project because I hadn't been burning any midnight oil on the FLARE software. I was ready to go and my boss gave me my next task: Build FLARE's rebuild process.

When a disk in the system failed, that failed disk would be pulled out from the chassis (live), and a healthy replacement would be re-inserted (live). My software would be instructed to rebuild, on the new disk, the data that would have been on the old disk if that old disk had not failed. I designed this software, held a design review, and wrote the code. Like my first task, I finished the new task ahead of schedule, too.

One of the members of our team left the company. He had been working on a piece of the FLARE software known as the configuration manager (CM). His unplanned departure put the project schedule in jeopardy. The CM was a key element to managing the disk array system we were building. My boss asked me to finish the job started by the team member who quit. I did. Ahead of schedule.

During this time, the hardware became ready, and we began running the FLARE software on the actual device itself. My RAID and rebuild algorithms ran without problems. We started measuring the performance of the system, and the numbers looked good. We discovered the mathematical calculations were slowing down the system, so my boss asked me to rewrite some of my software in the native language of the CPU.

Performance optimization is normally done after a product's first shipment to customers, but because I had completed all of my assignments ahead of schedule, I was available. We decided to modify the software and release a faster product.

The personal and corporate benefits of getting it done early are clear. My reputation among my team and, to some extent, within my department, was solid. The product we were building was running in the lab with high quality and high speed.

I had achieved a number of successes with the RAID project. I established a solid reputation as someone who can get things done. This sort of credibility is a great resource upon which to draw in the workforce. I didn't think about innovation but focused on quality and timeliness. The idea for the product was someone else's, but I figured out how to implement it and then improve its performance. I've often revisited this foundational project in my career and reflected on whether or not I am still known as a person who gets it done. I think I am and I'm glad of that. This type of person is influential.

After nine months of full-time work I had my first "idea." I had worked on all aspects of the FLARE code, using standard software development techniques, exercising creativity, and working hard. However, I had not been presented with any challenges or problems for which I didn't have a ready answer. In other words, I had not been asked to come up with any innovative solutions or novel ideas.

That all changed when a Data General VP showed up at my cubicle and asked me a fairly straightforward question. "Steve," he said, "are you confident that your software is correct? Is it ready to ship to customers?"

I looked him straight in the eye and told him, "No."

3. Illuminating that First Idea

I was confident in my software, but not confident enough to ship it. I had never been on a team that shipped a storage system before. I didn't have much experience with disk drive behavior. I didn't know what sorts of unpredictable behaviors might occur in the field. I wanted these flaws, whether caused by the product or triggered by some nefarious deed perpetrated by someone else's rogue software, to crop up so we could resolve them before we shipped the product. Until I tested the living daylights out of the software, I couldn't look management in the face and say, "Let's ship it."

This was my first opportunity to innovate, and it's a daunting lesson for anyone starting out in the industry. I could have looked at my boss (and my vice president) and said, "Help, I don't know what to do." Instead, I began a thought process, a sort of a three-legged stool, two legs of which were "knowns," and searched for an answer to that third leg, the "unknown." I have relied on this process throughout my career and it's rarely, if ever, failed me. Actually, it's not a three-legged stool; it's a modified Venn diagram (in a "traditional" Venn diagram, the components are known). I call this technique *Venn diagram innovation.*

I've labeled the three spheres in the Venn diagram as the customer sphere, the sphere of expertise, and the adjacent sphere. Innovation occurs when one successfully combines the three spheres in such a way as to create an overlap that uniquely solves a customer problem. Influence occurs when the owner of the adjacent sphere helps implement the idea and thus solves the customer problem.

I solved my crisis of confidence by following this approach. My thought process during that period illustrates perfectly this approach to innovation. Usually — but not always! — innovation is triggered by some action within the customer sphere.

The customer sphere represents the requirements of the customer. In the early 1980s, customers had some fairly simple requirements for their storage technology and a diagram of this sphere can be drawn fairly easily, as shown in figure 1.

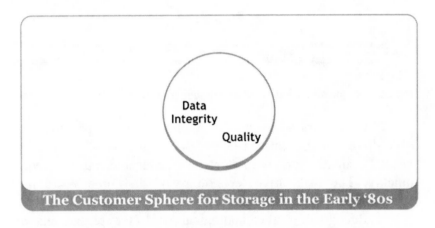

The Customer Sphere for Storage in the Early '80s

Figure 1. Storage in the early 1980s had simple requirements.

Customers wanted their disk drives to function well (the quality requirement) and they wanted them to return the right data (the data integrity requirement). The disk drive industry in this era was not sexy by any means. Disks were often described as fat, dumb, and slow. The CPUs attaching to those disks were sexy. Data General was one of the companies that prospered due, in part, to its CPU technology.

In the 1980s, CPU speeds increased; disk speeds could not keep pace. As shown in figure 2, this disparity added a new requirement into the customer sphere: performance.

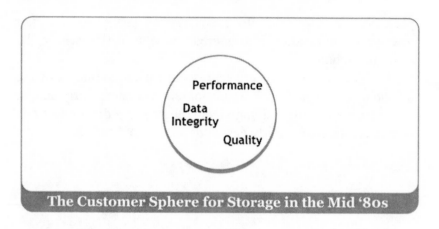

Figure 2. By the mid-1980s, customers required faster storage.

Customers were satisfied with the quality provided by disk drives in the early 1980s, but, by the mid-1980s, they needed their disk drives to store data faster and return it more quickly. The disk drive technology of that time could not accommodate these demands.

Recognizing a technological void, the researchers at UCal Berkeley responded by formalizing some of the newer ideas in the industry. "Gang together a group of disk drives and make them look and behave like one large disk," they recommended. "Use a technique called RAID to protect against the increased failure rates that will inevitably result from using so many disk drives," they added. They wrote a paper about this technique, and my first real assignment as a full-time employee was to build an implementation of the ideas from that paper.

The paper put forward a number of interesting concepts and theories, but it did not describe exactly how to build the RAID algorithms. The paper did not warn the industry about the very real risk to data integrity. Just because the customer sphere contained a new requirement (performance) did not mean the existing requirements (including data integrity) were no longer important. Consider the basic premise of the RAID algorithms, highlighted in figure 3. A CPU writes the consecutive values "1", "2", "3", and "4" to what it believes to be one very large disk drive. The CPU assumes that the very large disk drive is storing the data in contiguous areas on the disk.

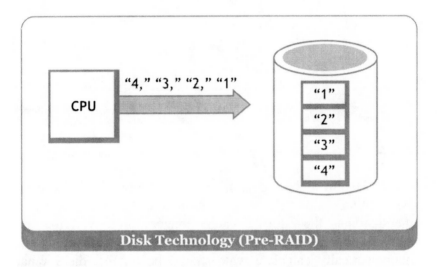

Figure 3. Information is placed in consecutive locations on one disk.

With RAID technology, the CPU still believes it is writing to one large disk, but in actuality, the data is being distributed across many disks and redundant information (parity) is calculated (and written) to protect against failures, as shown in figure 4 . For the sake of simplicity, I've used the basic mathematical function of addition to describe the parity value (many implementations instead use a mathematical technique known as "exclusive or," but that distinction isn't really germane to the topic).

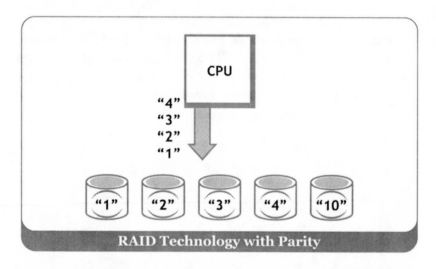

Figure 4. RAID technology with parity yields redundant information.

Herein is the problem: Let's assume the third disk dies. Because the value "3" was only written to that one disk, when that disk dies, the value "3" can no longer be retrieved from the surface of any disk in the system. RAID software must mathematically calculate what should be on that disk. What happens if the parity falls out of sync? What happens if adjacent disks experience errors, too? Myriad things could go wrong.

For the first time in the history of the storage industry, mainline storage software would mathematically recreate missing customer data on the fly.

The MD software I was subsequently tasked to create sat squarely in my sphere: the sphere of expertise from that original two-sphere Venn diagram of customer and expert (see figure 5). I had proven myself to be the worldwide expert in my own implementation of RAID. I knew the software inside and out. The problem presented by the customer's data integrity requirement was difficult to solve. How could I possibly be sure my software would never return the wrong data?

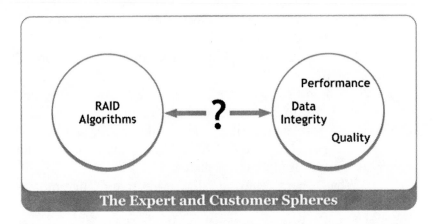

Figure 5. Two known spheres (expert and customer) in a Venn diagram.

This problem was my first opportunity to innovate with influence. The more I thought about the problem, the more I realized the solution would need to come from outside of my sphere of expertise. I would need to collaborate with others in order to achieve the desired outcome.

Data General's test engineering group was responsible for writing software that ensured product quality. This group operated, essentially, as a sphere of testing expertise adjacent to my own sphere of expertise and it had a testing framework supporting diagnostic tests that measured storage system quality, performance, and yes, data integrity. But this group had absolutely no idea how to conduct effective tests on my particular software algorithms. How could they write tests that visited each and every state of my RAID state machine?

I didn't know the answer, but I had an idea that this adjacent sphere of expertise could help. So I approached one of their software engineers, showed him my state machine diagrams, and explained the problem.

"Well," he said, "it seems to me that we're going to need some backdoor commands that inject faults into the system."

"Like what?" I asked.

"Like the ability to kill a disk drive," he responded matter-of-factly.

That didn't seem so hard. I knew the hardware team had added the ability to power on and power off any given disk drive. If the test engineering team could trigger a piece of software that powered off a disk at just the wrong time, it would cover quite a few of my internal states.

"What about causing disks to return intermittent failures?" I asked.

"I don't know," he responded. "Is there any way to corrupt the surface of the disk?"

I thought about that one. We actually appended parity (the extra failure checking data) to the end of every piece of customer data. We could corrupt this information, which would be very similar to a disk misbehaving. I had the answer to one of the testing engineer's questions. "Can you describe the data layout of the RAID algorithms? Can you report exactly where a disk is being rebuilt?"

The exchange continued in this manner, and we generated more creative ways to torture my software and verify the data integrity of my solution.

An idea was born, and this idea became known as the disk array qualifier (DAQ). The intersection of the three spheres of innovation had resulted in a new piece of software that solved the problem.

My boss and my vice president agreed with the approach, and the DAQ became a reality. A large number of test suites were written that powered off disk drives at the wrong time, corrupted data at the worst possible moment, flooded a disk with write commands as it was being rebuilt, wrote odd-sized files to span multiple disks, and performed more feats of mayhem. It was a truly innovative solution, and Figure 6 depicts how all three spheres came together to create this innovation.

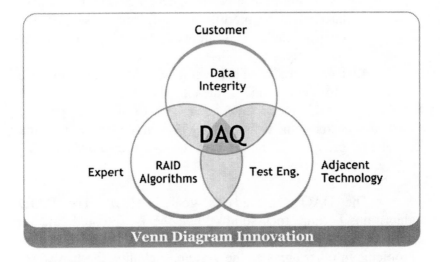

Figure 6. Solution based on the expert, customer, and adjacent technology.

The foundation of influence is demonstrating the ability to get it done, whatever it is. No sooner had I established this reputation than I encountered a problem I needed to solve. Once I had a problem to solve, I followed these steps to solve it:

1. I took the initiative to find an adjacent sphere. This was my first chance to prove I could innovate with others. I wasn't chasing an answer to someone else's idea. I exhibited a strong desire to collaborate on a solution and I owned the problem.

2. I shared creative control with the adjacent sphere (in many cases I have actually yielded control). I let my peer drive the solution. This allowed him to be creative and also own (or share ownership of) the problem.
3. I supported the adjacent sphere's efforts. I bent over backwards to modify my software to support the quality hooks that allowed the DAQ to test my RAID algorithms.
4. I gave credit where credit was due. I told my vice president —and I meant what I said — that we would never have been able to ship our product without the efforts of my peer in the test engineering group. We made sure he was rewarded for his efforts.

The DAQ achieved its goal in 1990. The RAID algorithms became rock-solid. When the DAQ could find no more data integrity problems in my software, it started to find problems in other areas of the system, including the hardware! It became a valuable system testing tool that improved quality beyond RAID.

As a result of comprehensive testing with the DAQ, we had built a RAID implementation that was fast and reliable: the original goal of the RAID paper. In the early 1990s, we sold dozens of disk arrays. We renamed the product CLARiiON® and started to sell thousands. The CLARiiON product developed into a brand known for being fast and reliable. Customers entrusted the brand with their most important data. In 1999, the largest and most successful storage company in the world (EMC) bought Data General for the sole purpose of acquiring the CLARiiON technology. Hundreds and thousands of CLARiiONs are in operation around the world, providing fast and reliable access to customer data.

The DAQ is still running in EMC's labs, torturing any new feature that tries to make it into customer's hands.

Is the DAQ the most influential idea I've been a part of? To this point, I'd have to say yes. We owned the problem, found the adjacent sphere, shared the creative wealth, and shipped the software that impacted the storage industry. This software has handled successfully literally trillions of requests to store the world's information.

In 1991, the same Data General VP showed up at my cubicle and asked me a familiar question. "Steve," he said, "are you confident that your software is correct? Is it ready to ship to customers?"

I looked him straight in the eye and said, "Yup."

4. Leading in the Trenches

One of the main reasons I have been able to drive innovation into new products is my calculated decision to stay in the trenches. I worked on the RAID algorithms for several years. Over the course of time, the size of our team grew as the success of the product increased. I started to feel restless working in my corner of the world.

Good work comes to those who get it done and I didn't need to wait long for a good project to find me.

Our product was out in the field, selling well. The RAID algorithms were providing fast and reliable storage. There were certain situations, however, in which our solution wasn't so fast and our customers let us know about them. When customers were frequently writing new information, and infrequently reading that information, they experienced a problem known as the RAID write penalty. Any time new data is written, four disk operations would occur: read the old data, write the new, read the old parity, write the new parity, as depicted in Figure 7.

.

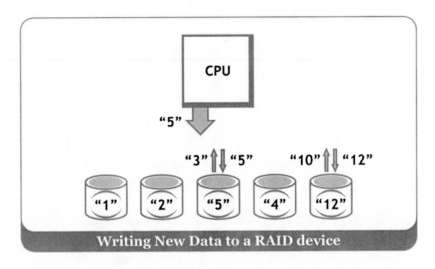

Figure 7. Writing new data to a RAID device is a four-step process.

If the customer writes data repeatedly to a RAID system, overall system performance is going to be very slow. Some of our customers were streaming data from a tape drive and sequentially storing the data onto our RAID implementation. Needless to say, with all that writing going on, they were not happy with the performance they were experiencing.

A solution to this particular problem would not be easy to build. Some disk drives had already implemented a technique known as *write caching*. A disk write cache places the new data temporarily in fast-access memory and permanently stores it later, when the disk is less busy. I had decided, as part of my RAID implementation, that I would never use disk write caching. It was too risky.

If write caching was too risky, what was the alternative? What about building our own cache above the disk drives? The concept, as sketched by my team and boss, is depicted in Figure 8.

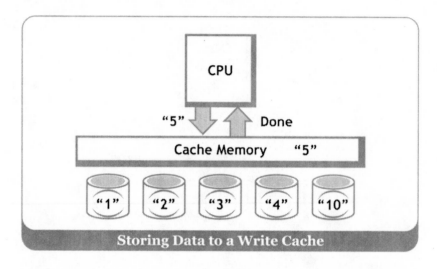

Figure 8. Storing data to a write cache hides the RAID write penalty.

This technique, while fast, jeopardizes data integrity. What happens if the memory fails? What happens during a power failure? The CPU has already been told that the operation is done, and therefore the system should always return the value "5" and never return the value currently on disk ("3").

Collectively, the team decided we needed to build a battery-backed, mirrored write cache. The battery would protect against power failures, while the mirroring of the memory would protect against memory failures.

Building mirrored write cache software would be enormously complex. Testing the solution would be complex. Adding a battery to the hardware would be complex. Coordinating all of the different teams to build this system would be complex. Still, our customers — one of the spheres critical to Venn diagram innovation — had a problem and we, as representatives of the expert sphere, needed to come up with a solution. We elevated the proposal for this new solution to the company leadership.

I was asked to take the lead for building a write cache product. I did not accept the assignment immediately. Saying yes to this project meant that I would no longer be focusing on writing software day in and day out. I would still be building software in the sense that I would be participating in the construction of a software solution. I had a strong desire to do something new. After thinking it over for a few days, I accepted.

Looking back now, I realize this decision dramatically increased my influence. Was the idea for a write cache innovative? No. It had been done before. Would our implementation of a mirrored write cache be innovative? Yes, and leading this project put me squarely in a position to take another innovative idea and influence a delivery to customers.

Let me simply skip to the bottom line: we shipped a mirrored write cache RAID device in 1994. As we had done with the first RAID device, we made our mirrored write cache RAID faster without sacrificing data integrity. During the development of this device, I made a significant discovery about how to increase personal influence. It's a leadership theme that goes beyond getting the job done and targets precisely how to win the trust of a larger number of co-workers.

Do the jobs that nobody else wants to do.

One of my main roles as a project lead was to shield the team from the mundane tasks that kept them from making progress on the actual building of the write cache software.

In order to truly innovate with influence, I had to give up the hands-on work and take on the role of a servant leader. What does a servant leader do? He leads by serving the needs of his team.

For example, the quality team wanted a design specification from the engineer building the actual write cache software. I wrote it instead, so that the developer could keep coding.

The hardware team wanted our platform engineer to present a discussion on the behavior of the software while the battery was charging. I handled it for him.

The performance team wanted to model how fast the write cache would perform. I generated a presentation describing how it would work.

The test engineers were finding bugs during our first release. I resolved any bugs they found so the team could continue its forward momentum.

I took every request from every group and applied the get-it-done-early principle. I wrote design specs that exceeded expectations and delivered them a week early. I gave a presentation to another group after letting its members preview what I was about to say so I knew they'd be receptive and fully satisfied. I responded immediately to every request for my time or that of my team so my team could succeed.

As I write this chapter, I am working in a group of more than 150 people, overseeing the creation of a 500-page system specification that nobody wants to write but everybody wants to read. This is a job for a leader, and leaders have a much better chance of delivering their innovative solutions.

I have experienced numerous benefits as a result of choosing to lead:

1. My visibility has grown well beyond my own group.
2. My reputation as someone who gets it done has spread.
3. My efforts have been appreciated by my co-workers as well as my managers.

This last point about gratitude is fundamental to influence. My co-workers in the trenches were grateful for my having taken on some of the more mundane jobs so they could focus on what they loved to do.

The next time I brought an idea their way, they would listen, and they would want to help.

That's influence.

I learned that staying in the trenches is a key choice for an intrapreneur, because that's where innovative ideas will ultimately be built.

Shipping a mirrored write cache product meant I had been part of another innovative team whose efforts had once again shaped the storage industry. No other company had ever shipped a mirrored write cache inside of a storage system. My product was on the rise, and I was on the verge of some serious recognition for my particular contributions.

So I left.

5. Overcoming the Innovator's Dilemma

Every time I got it done, I had a choice to make. What would I do next? I needed a new task. Each time I was presented with a new task, I asked myself, "What do I want to be when I grow up?"

I can see now that I always wanted to build something cool. I wanted to hear about something that customers really, really wanted, and then build a great product that met the need. Usually, when I reached this intersection, I had four possible choices. I believe that two of them are good choices for an intrapreneur, and two of them are not.

The flowchart in Figure 9 illustrates my point. A flowchart is a common tool of the trade for software engineers. Nerds love to create them. Using flowcharts may make you appear smarter than you actually are. This is to your benefit and will increase your influence. Use them frequently.

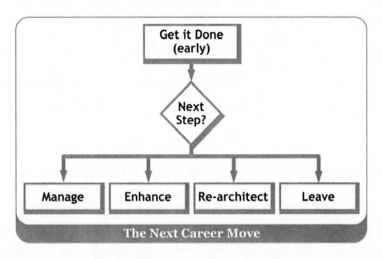

Figure 9. Four possible options for the next career move.

Influence: Overcoming the Innovator's Dilemma

For innovators who desire to influence, the two choices on the left (manage and enhance) are steps to a slippery slope.

I have never assumed the role of a manager. Nobody has ever reported to me, I have never put together a budget, and I have never ordered equipment. I am perfectly happy to have never done these things. The reason for this is that I always knew what I wanted to do: I wanted to build things. I've had some great managers over the years who have enabled me to build things and some of them have also provided outstanding career guidance.

Becoming a line manager (running a small or medium-sized team) may be an excellent choice for some. A line manager should, by virtue of the title of manager, shift the focus from innovation to team empowerment. A manager who gets it done does not (and should not) champion individual ideas. Trying to do so can yield disastrous results:

1. The team (and its goal) can suffer as the manager spends time on the idea and not the people.
2. The innovative builders on the team are robbed of their ability to develop a reputation of being able to lead in the trenches, where influence and true innovation are formed.

I've seen several line managers attempt to innovate with influence. Usually, the results are always the same: both the team and the idea lose. Is it possible for a line manager to also be an intrapreneur? Certainly. But it is a challenging line to walk.

The second career choice innovators should avoid is what I call the path of enhancement. Enhancement refers to the concept of making small or minor modifications to an area of expertise. Some people love this activity and stay with it for

41

years. They love the continual improvement and strive to build their creation to a more perfect state.

I strolled down this path once and I was absolutely miserable.

We had shipped the first version of our RAID product. The quality and data integrity of the product were outstanding. We were able to survive and recover from single failures of any component in the system, whether it was a disk, a power supply, a fan, a CPU, or even the software itself. We decided to improve the product by adding the ability to recover from certain double failures that our customers might experience.

I've already recounted my work with data parity and how the RAID algorithms could read customer data even when the disk storing that customer data has failed. One of RAID's most attractive benefits is that customers can continue to write new data in the face of a disk failure. Consider the scenario depicted in figure 10.

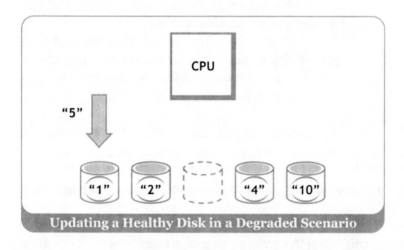

Figure 10. RAID algorithms enable storing data in a degraded scenario.

In this scenario, a disk is missing (it should contain the value "3") and the customer is changing the value "1" to the value "5." This should result in the parity value being changed from "10" to "14." There's a big problem here. What happens in the case of a power failure? The value "10" never gets updated, and therefore the value on the "missing" disk could be calculated incorrectly.

We knew about this problem before we ever shipped our first product, and we put safeguards in place so that we never returned incorrect data. Instead, we returned an error code that basically meant, "Sorry, but the value you're reading has been lost."

In other words, if a customer experienced a disk failure, and then experienced a power outage, that customer might experience data loss if write operations were in progress. We decided to solve this problem with an innovative technique called *parity shedding*, as depicted in figure 11.

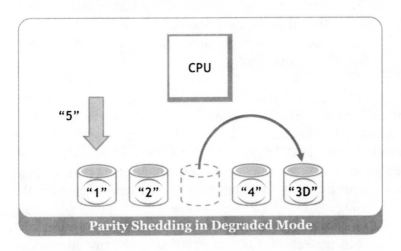

Figure 11. Parity shedding in degraded mode protects against data loss.

Influence: Overcoming the Innovator's Dilemma

Whenever the RAID software received a write operation and was aware that a disk had previously failed, it first re-created the data on the failed disk, then moved it over to the parity location, and then marked it as data (D) instead of parity. The new value could then be written. This effectively prevented data loss during a degraded scenario.

Somebody had to modify the RAID software, and that somebody was me. I retrieved my state machines and design specifications and dove in. I worked on new tests for the DAQ. I modified my original state machine software. I had done all of these things before and now I was doing them again. I took the work seriously and I got it done. As a matter of fact, I got it done early.

But it was a grind. I was extremely unhappy, and I didn't know why. Looking back now, I learned two valuable lessons:

1. I had a passion for inventing that was not being satisfied through enhancement.
2. I had sufficient influence to request that someone else do the work.

This second point is very, very important. I was not locked into my job description forever. As an inexperienced employee, I reasoned that because I had poured so much of myself into the RAID algorithms, I was the only one who would be able to modify them. I was wrong. Any talented person could have stepped into a situation such as this and taken over the work, using my thorough pseudo-code and comprehensive state machines. Some people love to take an existing project and tinker it to perfection. Case in point: some of my co-workers who joined me on the RAID algorithms are still at it 15 years later!

I'm glad the situation unfolded the way that it did; being miserable helped me to learn what I liked and what I didn't. And I'm proud to have taken the job seriously enough to get it done, because parity shedding made a big difference to our customers.

When I met with customers who were evaluating products from our competitors, I told them the story about parity shedding.

"These are the lengths we go to in order to protect your data," I told them. "What's our competitor going to do?"

It wasn't a hard sell. It didn't need to be. And we would win nearly every sale.

I already knew a career as a manager was not for me. During the parity shedding project, I learned the career choice of "enhancement" was not for me, either.

This brings me to the two choices I always consider when I'm ready to move on to my next task. Do I re-architect or do I leave?

After finishing and shipping the parity shedding enhancement for Data General, and feeling thoroughly miserable about my life enhancing software, my phone rang.

It was EMC.

6. Choosing to Stay or Go

Given my decision not to manage and my dissatisfaction with the process of enhancing existing products, I've proposed that innovators should choose between one of two paths upon project completion: re-architect or leave. I've followed the re-architect path several times, and I've decided to leave several times. Knowing which path to choose and when to choose it can be an art. I didn't have a set plan and I know of no particular rules to help an innovator make that decision. Looking back, I can see that I made my choices according to a gut feeling about the amount of innovation each of these two choices offered. Sometimes it's not a straightforward choice.

Right after I completed the parity shedding modification, a headhunter called me at Data General. This particular headhunter was recruiting for a growing company called EMC. Like Data General, EMC, whose headquarters was located about 10 miles away from my office at Data General, built and shipped a storage device. EMC's device was called Symmetrix® ("Symm" for short). The Symm device was much larger than Data General's RAID system. Because of the size disparity, the two products really didn't compete with each other in the marketplace at that time.

The headhunter had found my number somehow—headhunters rarely, if ever, reveal their sources — and he called me at just the right time. I was restless after finishing the parity shedding project. I had made incremental enhancements to my work and hadn't enjoyed the experience. The headhunter's pitch was quite good. Not only was EMC offering a big salary increase, but the company's revenue and stock price were already on a fantastic growth curve. It never hurts to consider one's options, so I drove down to 171 South Street in Hopkinton, Massachusetts, for an interview.

No sooner did I walk in the door than I was escorted to Dick Egan's office. That's Egan, as in the "E" of EMC.

"I know you're not looking for work," he told me, "but let me tell you about how great this company's about to be." He went on to expound, in glowing terms, on how EMC was about to become THE provider of storage solutions.

Talk about a visionary! He was absolutely right. So, where would I fit in?

"We need this RAID technology," he said, "and we understand you're the one who knows how to build it."

Although EMC had implemented portions of the RAID technology, they had not implemented the particular flavor of RAID (known as RAID-5) I had worked on at Data General. In addition to the speed and reliability benefits of RAID-5, the parity technique saved customers a significant amount of money (as opposed to EMC's implementation of RAID on Symmetrix).

EMC had hired a headhunter and told him to look around for storage software engineers. Apparently, EMC also suggested the headhunter try looking within Data General. This hint led to my eventual interview.

I left Dick's office and completed the interview circuit with other members of EMC. Everyone had stayed late to meet with me. As I spoke with people, it became very clear to me that I was not being interviewed. I was being recruited.

Within days, I was offered a 30% raise and 2,000 shares of 1992 EMC stock options. EMC wanted RAID-5 technology and was willing to reward me in order to get it.

I thought about the offer and ended up turning it down.

Two months later, Dick Egan called my house and asked if I'd reconsider.

I said no.

During this process, I thought about why my instinct had been to reject his offer, not once but twice. I realized I wanted to create something new. I wanted to build something innovative, something that nobody else had done before. I didn't want to leave one position for another position where I was being asked to recreate a previous success. So I stuck with Data General.

The option to "re-create" may be attractive for some. These folks might love to redo a previous project from scratch. They might remember previous mistakes and welcome the opportunity to benefit from that experience.

Not me.

Shortly thereafter, when I was offered the project leadership position on the mirrored write cache project, I was intrigued. As I have already mentioned, nobody in the industry had built a mirrored write cache. Building the software for this solution would require a major re-architecture of our system. I took that job at Data General instead of jumping to EMC to re-create RAID-5. It turned out to be a valuable lesson on choosing the right next step in an innovative career.

Re-architecting my work to introduce brand-new functionality was a valid career choice for me. It was work that was neither enhancement nor improvement. I was working on a complex, never-done-before challenge. The opportunity to design a mirrored write cache, combined with the opportunity to develop trench leadership experience, resulted in a clear decision. Don't leave; re-architect.

When I was done with the mirrored write cache (as in shipped with high quality), I left the FLARE team. I actually left *before* the product started to hit the big time revenue-wise (this can be a common occurrence for an innovator). The speed of the write cache, coupled with the data integrity provided by the RAID algorithms, attracted a very large customer: Hewlett-

Packard (HP). Data General built a relationship with HP, and HP sold thousands of CLARiiON devices.

I decided to leave because the work in front of me fell into the category of enhancements. The write cache was going to be modified to function as a read cache as well. Faster, larger disk drives were being added to the system. Customers were asking for video streaming capabilities with improved performance. All of these projects were interesting, but none of them qualified as a significant re-architecture. This was why I decided to leave.

There was only one problem.

I had nowhere to go.

Data General was (at its heart) a server company. It was also a company that wasn't growing in terms of entirely new technologies, in spite of the fact that the CLARiiON product line was growing by leaps and bounds. I didn't want to stay on the CLARiiON team, but I didn't want to transfer anywhere else within Data General either, because the way I saw it, the future in the rest of the company wasn't so bright.

Fortunately for me, at this time, CLARiiON had begun an investment in an adjacent sphere of technology: The CLARiiON Systems Engineering group. As far as I could tell, the charter of this group was to work on technologies that attach to a CLARiiON. A CLARiiON could attach to servers from different vendors, such as Sun or IBM. The Systems Engineering group was tasked with ensuring these attachments performed without a hitch. They had also hired a set of contractors to build a management interface to CLARiiON. As more and more customers were buying CLARiiON, these customers were demanding more sophisticated tools to manage the product itself.

The group seemed to be a hodge-podge of engineering talent with backgrounds all over the map. They had hired a brand-new engineering manager from the non-CLARiiON side of Data General and were about to bring in a new vice president to run the whole operation.

It seemed to me that, over time, this group would become pivotal to the future of CLARiiON. I went through a round of interviews. The engineering manager and the vice president indicated that, were I to join the team, I would likely have the opportunity to create a new storage management architecture from scratch.

I was sold. I left my old team and joined the new one, essentially relocating to an adjacent sphere of technology.

I was the domain expert when it came to storage system internals, but I knew nothing about building software for managing storage systems. The two technologies are adjacent — the management architecture sends command and control messages to the storage system — but they are not identical and being an expert in one technology doesn't necessarily translate to automatic expertise in another. In time, with hard work, this limitation would be overcome.

I was in a new group, but I maintained close relationships with previous teams. In other words, I maintained a level of influence with my previous team, while building additional influence with a new set of people. I widened my domain of knowledge (becoming an expert in two spheres), while simultaneously widening my domain of influence. The wider one's domain of influence, the greater the opportunity to succeed as an intrapreneur.

Sounds good, doesn't it? Of course, there's a catch.

I got a lot of strange looks when I joined this new team. Many of my co-workers on the old team wondered why I would leave such a critically visible position as a key player for a product that was on the rise. RAID algorithms and write cache software were cool, sexy technologies. Storage management software wasn't. If the RAID algorithms fail, you lose access to data. If your management software fails, you just restart it! Where's the challenge in that?

My first project in the group was to write the first-ever CLARiiON command line interface (called CLARCLI, soon to be known as NAVICLI).

As I had done many years earlier, when I first joined Data General as a full-time employee, I sat down and wrote a diagram of my software.

I opened up a design specification and wrote down the CLI syntax.

I held a design review.

I wrote the code. I got it done. (I finished early, too.)

I worked with the test organization to make sure it was high quality.

We shipped it to customers and they began using it. (They're still using it a dozen years later).

What happened next? I took a trench leadership position and began building a new product with a group of about fifteen engineers. It would take a few years to finish.

During that time, my overall corporate visibility faded. I was no longer "the man," the most recognizable of individuals building the red-hot CLARiiON software internals.

This is good.

Visibility can be a bad thing.

7. Navigating Visibility

When it comes to implementing innovative ideas, visibility can help, but visibility can also hurt.

At the time I was building the quality hooks into my RAID algorithms as part of the DAQ innovation years earlier, very few people knew who I was. I was left undisturbed for weeks. The same thing could be said regarding my tenure on the write cache project. During those projects, my low profile (lack of visibility) helped me.

In 2003, this was still true. I had very little visibility at the corporate level. I was collaborating, innovating, and loving it. One day, I was summoned to the office of a high-level manager, who proceeded to thank me for everything I had done and then transferred me to a group that I didn't want to work for. The exact same thing had happened to me in 2006. In this case, lack of visibility hurt me. I lost direct access to the innovation I was driving.

As a result of being transferred, I learned about the different types of visibility and their benefits and risks. Navigating and controlling my own visibility has been challenging. I realized there are three important types of visibility:

1. *Horizontal visibility* refers to my visibility among the large number of people that are working in the trenches of my company.
2. *Executive visibility* refers to my visibility among the executive officers at my corporation.
3. *Vertical visibility* refers to visibility by my direct chain of management.

Influence: Navigating Visibility

In order to champion innovative ideas and have a positive impact on the corporation at large, I've developed a strategy to optimize each type of visibility:

- I strive to maximize my horizontal visibility.
- I strive to minimize my executive visibility.
- I strive to limit my vertical visibility to two levels above me (which I define as *plus-2* visibility).

I believe leading from within the trenches is the proper way to grow horizontal visibility. As a leader, I became more visible to the employees who benefited from my particular style of servant leadership. I also interacted with the people in the trenches of other organizations, which served to expand my sphere of influence. We got it done, and this success built even more influence. As part of my strategy to master the innovator's dilemma, I continually moved into adjacent spheres of technology, delivered ideas with new people, and maintained interaction with previous teams.

Throughout my career in various groups at Data General, I established a track record of productivity and built strong relationships. The next time I had a great idea, I had an open door to dozens, hundreds, or even thousands of people who remembered our joint experience as a positive one. It is highly likely that not only will they want to hear the idea, but they will also be open to sharing their own input into how best to get it done. They will want to help get it done, because the last time we worked together, we were successful. They benefited and the company benefited. This kind of influence can't be bought and it is absolutely invaluable.

In 2000, I left my group (again) and started over (again). Data General was acquired by EMC. After six successful years of building a new storage management product line

(Navisphere®), I came face to face (again) with the innovator's dilemma: should I stay or should I go? For the first time in my career, I was actually working for a company specializing in storage systems (EMC). I decided that if I transferred to EMC proper, I could find an adjacent sphere and design something new.

One of the recent inventions I was leaving behind me was my work on the storage area network (SAN). The CLARiiON team had shipped one of the first mid-range SANs in the industry, and I had been right in the thick of it. In a SAN, the storage device becomes the center of the universe; the servers tap into it and share available capacity. By sharing of available capacity, I don't necessarily mean that these servers can share each other's information, but rather that they can carve up their own dedicated portion of the storage. This concept is depicted in figure 12.

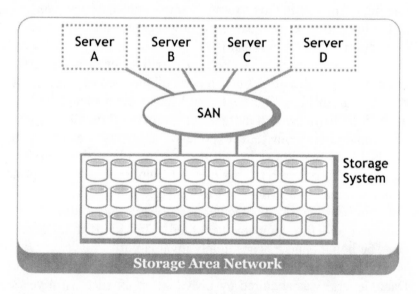

Figure 12. A storage area network (SAN) allows servers to share capacity.

As depicted in figure 12, each server attaches to a SAN and stores information in what appears to be a dedicated storage system. Each server remains blissfully unaware that the storage is actually managed across a much larger system shared by many servers.

In 2000, very large SANs were being built and customers were beginning to ask for tools to keep track of the sharing of storage. To be more precise, they were asking for billing and reporting software. EMC did not have such a product. I had no experience with billing and reporting software, but I was already an expert in the SAN domain. So, once again, I decided to leave my familiar team and my comfortable little (but always expanding) sphere of influence and join an adjacent sphere of technology in a different EMC facility located in the not-far-away town of Hopkinton.

The group I joined was a research group. When I say "research," I mean they started projects but they did not finish them. This was a new role for me: I was not leading anyone, nor was I in the trenches delivering a product, and this posed a problem. For the first time in my professional career, I could imagine an idea but not build. Not only would I not build it, but it was entirely possible that nobody would build it! I would, at best, be able to create a software framework for a billing and reporting system and hope the idea had wings to fly on its own.

This is where horizontal visibility came into play. After thirteen years of building influence and moving from one group to another, I met up again with two former co-workers who were looking for an adjacent sphere of their own. They agreed to come on board and build the product. I handed them the design specifications, and off they went to build the product. Within eighteen months, they had released a product known as StorageScope^{TM}. StorageScope was the first product I had worked on outside of the CLARiiON organization. It went on to become a successful product and, as storage industry customers adopt *cloud storage* (which delivers storage as a service instead of hardware), I remain convinced that large companies will use StorageScope to create reports and bill customers that are sharing cloud storage capacity.

When I transferred from Data General to EMC, my executive visibility fell to zero. Executive visibility does not necessarily transfer when one transitions from an acquired company "up" to the parent organization. I was starting over, even though I had not actually left the company. Upper management in Hopkinton was not interested in a software engineer working on a billing and reporting tool. I was also out of sight and out of mind from the executives in my previous organization.

This lack of executive visibility wasn't such a bad thing. It allowed me to get the job done. I realized several benefits to having minimal executive visibility:

1. The higher my visibility by corporate executives, the more time I will be expected to spend with them in meetings.
2. The more time I spend in corporate-level meetings, the less time I have to get things done in the trenches.
3. Corporate executives tend to hold meetings well after quitting time.

While the first two points are self-explanatory, the last point deserves more elaboration. The greatest solutions to the toughest problems often come after "getting away from it all." I made a decision, very early in my career, to develop the habit of leaving work at the same time each day. This has become more difficult as my executive visibility has grown. I love the innovative process and tolerate the executive visibility, controlling the visibility as much as I can so that I have more time to innovate and deliver, while still having time for my family and myself.

This recommendation to eschew executive visibility may run against the corporate grain. Some folks may opt to innovate with influence for the sole purpose of receiving corporate attention. That's fine; it's their choice. Just be aware that if you desire the opportunity for continual innovation throughout your career, corporate recognition may stand in the way. Recognition can act like a magnet, pulling you out of the trenches.

You can make your choices with forethought or you can float along with the currents. I've worked carefully to be able to make my own decisions and I've had to make trade-offs. The satisfaction that results from continual innovation often comes with the price of a certain amount of anonymity. A savvy innovator will continually leave his creation and start over from scratch, sometimes in a place where he or she is completely unknown. I've recently come to realize that my company has made the decision to simultaneously recognize innovators and leave them alone. This is a perfect scenario for someone like me. It promotes influence and supports innovation.

There are risks associated with minimizing executive visibility. In 2003, I was reassigned to a group whose work did not appeal to me. My lack of executive visibility made me vulnerable to someone else's whims. I was able to recapture my fate and make different arrangements for myself, thanks to my relative high degree of horizontal visibility and influence, and I transferred to an organization whose work better suited my personal and professional needs.

In 2006, in my very first meeting with a corporate executive in my management chain, I was again assigned to a different organization without being asked. I didn't have enough of a relationship with this executive to be involved in the decision. In this particular case, I evaluated the new organization's potential for innovation and chose to make the transition.

The bottom line is that leaving the safety of innovative success, while eventually increasing influence, usually left me vulnerable. What is the best way to counter this vulnerability? The answer can be found in managing vertical visibility.

In 2003, my plus-2 management visibility was weak. I was, in essence, invisible, and this was not a good thing. By the year 2006, my vertical visibility was better — my immediate manager knew who I was and what I could do, and I knew he knew — but my relationship with my manager's manager — was not. My manager's manager did not know what I wanted and chose to make decisions for me. I am convinced that, if I had built a strong relationship with both levels of management above me, the message from upper management would have been different; I would have been given the option to choose my next position and not simply been assigned to a role that might not suit me.

Based on these experiences, I have taken care to maintain an accurate assessment of my vertical and executive visibility. I find that interaction is a good gauge of visibility and I work to maintain satisfactory visibility at both the vertical and executive levels. This is the current state of my visibility with these various levels:

- Level 1: Director: Excellent
- Level 2: Vice President: Excellent
- Level 3: Vice President: None
- Level 4: Senior Vice President: Rarely
- Level 5: Executive Vice President: None
- Level 6: President: None

Influence: Navigating Visibility

I believe my current situation is ideal for me. I refer to this situation as having good plus-2 visibility. I am six levels away from the top of the company; therefore I should create strong working relationships with the level 5 and level 4 managers. Most employees already know they should build a strong relationship with their immediate manager. I've also decided to have the same strong relationship with my manager's manager (who, in my case, is a VP).

My VP can do two things for me:

1. Influence other organizations within the company. This is especially important if I have an idea that requires resources in adjacent organizations; my VP may have a better chance of making it happen than I would because he has influence and political clout.
2. Protect the innovator. Once my VP becomes aware that I am an innovator with a track record for delivering high-quality results, I have someone who can look out for me during reorganizations and company transitions.

This approach may not work in all cases; it is highly dependent on the influence of my VP. I do believe, however, that it is a solid strategy for an innovator.

My final point on visibility has to do with social media. After twenty years in the storage industry, I had very little executive visibility, strong plus-2 vertical visibility, and a decent base of horizontal visibility within my own (and previous) organizations. With the advent of a social media platform within EMC (known as EMC ONE), my horizontal visibility has grown enormously (because I have chosen to become actively involved in this platform).

As a result of my significant horizontal visibility, my executive visibility has also grown, but mainly among those executives who make use of these social media tools. This type of exposure has been manageable; executives that communicate via Web 2.0 technologies can interact anytime and anywhere via the Web.

As a direct result of social media, innovators (and their ideas) can extend influence over a global sphere. My stories (blogs) about historical innovation have been well received and, as a result, my peers in trenches all around the globe have become receptive to innovative collaboration. This is fantastic. Intrapreneurs thrive when they can collaborate with each other in the trenches.

Should innovators leave the trenches?

That's a great question which, of course, leads me to another story.

8. Leaving the Trenches

After thirteen consecutive years of delivering CLARiiON technology, I chose to leave the trenches. I transferred to the mother ship at EMC Hopkinton. Emerging Technologies, the group I joined, was also sometimes called Advanced Development. This group did not fully develop and ship products. One of its roles, however, was to start products and hand them off to development teams. This group didn't get things done per se, at least not according to my definition of done.

Was it a mistake to move into this role? No. Did I lose the ability to generate innovative new ideas? No. Did I lose the ability to influence the shipment of these innovative ideas? Not entirely, but I would soon discover that, by leaving the trenches, my influence lessened. The trade-off of having joined a research group soon became clear. I learned about many new adjacent spheres and increased my expertise in those spheres. I found, however, that functioning in a research role changed my immediate impact.

EMC had acquired my former employer, Data General, and immediately decreed a six-month moratorium on transfers to EMC proper. The reasoning behind the moratorium was to not disrupt CLARiiON. In the meantime, I had reached a crossroads. After six years of innovation and delivery in my sphere of expertise (storage management), I had to make the decision to re-architect or leave.

The Navisphere project I was working on was about to undergo a major re-architecture. The software itself was going to be completely rewritten to run inside a Web browser, and the communication protocols between the browser and the CLARiiON itself were going to fundamentally change. I was in the middle of researching this re-architecture. Professionally, I knew continuing on this path was the right direction for me to follow, but personally, I felt as though I wouldn't learn anything new. So I waited out the six months and then left. I worked on my first task — proposed the StorageScope project, recruited some great guys to help build it, and off they went — and didn't look back.

Isn't that what being an intrapreneur is all about?

In this particular case, I do believe that by eventually bringing with me several top-notch developers who I knew could get it done, I was still exerting considerable influence in the completion of that product.

While my experience with StorageScope was, all in all, positive, my next project was a different story.

EMC ships a product known as PowerPath®. PowerPath is a piece of software that runs outside of a storage array and searches for different routing paths to send information to a storage system. PowerPath can use these different paths to increase performance, or it can use these different paths to navigate around failures that might occur on the route to the storage system. Figure 13 highlights the value of PowerPath.

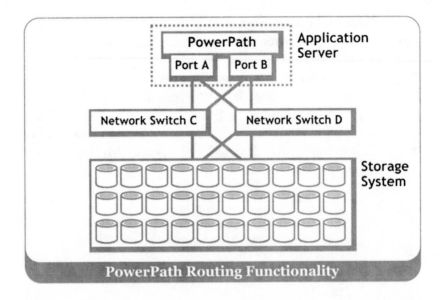

Figure 13. PowerPath's routing functionality adds value to storage systems.

PowerPath runs on an application server that consumes storage provided by a storage array. In the example depicted in figure 13, the customer has also installed redundant network switches in order to connect the server to the storage network. When an application wished to read data, for example, PowerPath could choose to send the request via port A and switch C, port A with switch D, port B with switch C, or port B with switch D. PowerPath can also sense failures along a given path and stop using that particular route until it is repaired.

Customers configured their environment this way to ensure high availability; extra hardware was purchased so that applications could ride through path failures. PowerPath remains a great product in this regard.

My Advanced Development team had some ideas about how to innovate with PowerPath. We decided to extend

PowerPath to become aware of a feature known as *storage array mirroring*. Mirroring provides an alternate copy of the data in case something goes wrong with the primary copy. Storage array mirroring software mirrored data from a primary storage array to a secondary storage array. EMC shipped mirroring software known as SRDF®. My team reasoned that PowerPath could sit on top of both storage arrays (instead of on top of just one), as depicted in Figure 14, and realize performance improvements.

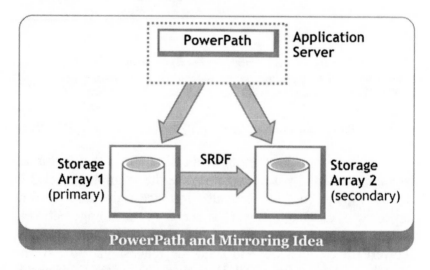

Figure 14. Mirroring and PowerPath could increase performance.

Figure 14 does not include the detailed routing and path circuitry in order to focus instead on the concept of mirroring. Normally, PowerPath focused its algorithmic attention on the primary array (e.g. Storage Array 1) only. All read and write requests were sent to the primary array. Well, if the secondary array contained an exact duplicate of the data on the primary array, why not take advantage of that fact by sending some read requests to that system? On paper, this proposed technique would prove to be faster, we theorized.

The PowerPath team had an office in Cambridge, Massachusetts, and they willingly showed me how to extend their software to perform this new trick. Their software was quite easy to work with. I quickly built a prototype and ran some performance benchmarks. My first test realized a performance gain of 10%.

Rethinking the PowerPath software to take advantage of storage array mirroring is an outstanding example of innovation. We took a problem in the customer domain (performance), became experts in a new sphere (PowerPath), and then combined it with an adjacent technology (disk array mirroring). The result, represented in figure 15, is called *mirrored pathing*.

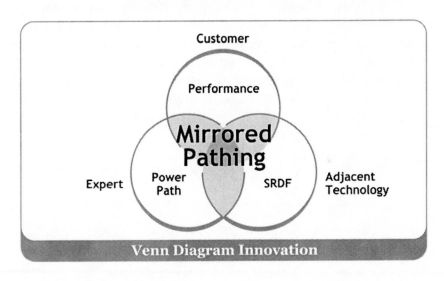

Figure 15. Another solution created via Venn Diagram Innovation.

The theory was great, but we encountered a problem when we tried to productize this idea. The PowerPath team was a friendly bunch of folks and our collaboration had been successful, but I had zero influence with them at this point. I was simply a researcher building an experiment. As a result, the idea died. Mirrored pathing didn't make it into customer hands.

This was a first for me and I found it frustrating. Would it have helped if I had built a closer relationship with the PowerPath team (without actually being on the team)? I soon had the chance to find out.

One of the bigger problems customers face is *data migration*. For any number of reasons, customers may choose to move their information off of one storage array and onto a different one. This migration is complicated and can result in *downtime*: customer applications are shut down while their information is moved from one system to another.

EMC wanted an easier migration solution for its customers. PowerPath seemed to be a great way to solve this migration problem because not only did it run on the same machine as the customers' application, but it also had visibility and access to a variety of different migration technologies. Consider the PowerPath data migration solution depicted in Figure 16.

Influence: Leaving the Trenches

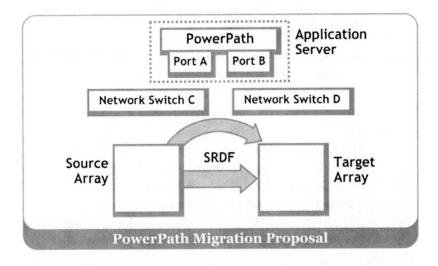

Figure 16. A solution providing multiple online migration options.

The beauty of this diagram is that PowerPath could actually choose from one of three different ways to perform online migration of information with minimal (or perhaps no) disruption to the customer. If the source and target arrays could use SRDF, the data could be migrated directly between the storage systems. If the network switches had the intelligence to migrate the data, they could do the job. Finally, if PowerPath realized it had no other options, it could copy the information from the source array to the target array by reading from one port and writing to another.

There were too few resources in EMC's Cambridge facility to build this software (they were busy working on other PowerPath features). I was instructed to commute into Cambridge and work side by side with the team on the design of a solution. After several months, we found some top-notch developers in Cork, Ireland, who joined the team. A project leader emerged from that group as well. Within nine months, we had built a proof of concept. We flew some of the team from Cork to the United States, gathered together some of the top field engineers, and showed them a demonstration of PowerPath Data Migration. They were blown away. It was exactly what they were looking for.

More people were hired. My work was done, and I was reassigned.

And then it stalled.

It was frustrating, but if there was one thing I knew, it was that the customer problem would not go away. And sure enough, several years later, the team in Cambridge dusted off the solution built in Cork, reworked some of the assumptions, and shipped a data migration product known as PowerPath Data Migration Enabler.

My participation in a research group ended in 2003. My ability to influence during my three-year ride resulted in two new products and both expanded and increased my expertise with EMC's product portfolio. Looking back, that time period felt like going back to school, but I also felt that being disconnected from the trenches (where the real work of creating products is done) had its drawbacks. When my research group disbanded in July 2003, I had no choice but to leave for yet another organization.

I decided to head back to the trenches and used my own influence to do just that.

9. Chasing the Light Bulb

EMC is a large company, due in part to the incredible number of acquisitions (roughly forty companies) it has completed this decade. It's a wonderful environment for an innovator, because it provides many adjacent spheres for those desiring a perpetually fresh experience with new technology.

How does one choose a group to join? Which organization would be the best one to move to? These are key career decisions for any innovator, and my advice is to do what I did in 2003: I chased the light bulb.

One of the companies EMC purchased was a Belgian company, Filepool. Filepool created Internet-based software that ran on distributed servers. The Filepool team joined its new EMC co-workers to create a product known as Centera®. Centera was a new type of storage system. I was considering joining the Centera team, but I had already built a storage system. I was skeptical as to whether working as part of the Centera team would allow me to learn anything new. The group was hiring and I happened to be at yet another crossroads in search of a new position, so I decided to take a look.

The storage systems with which I was familiar were known as *block storage* systems. Blocks of information would be created by applications. This information would flow through software such as PowerPath, leave the ports on an application server, flow into a SAN across network switches, and eventually arrive at the storage system with a set of instructions. In the block storage world, these instructions would be along the lines of "store these blocks of information in location *xyz*," where *xyz* would be a number such as 100, 1000, or 10000, for example.

Another common type of storage system, *file storage*, didn't respond to block requests, but instead responded to file requests, such as "create a new folder," "open a file," or "delete a file." The differences between these two traditional storage systems are highlighted in figure 17.

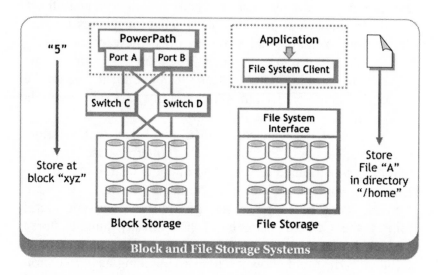

Figure 17. An overview of block storage and file storage systems.

As I was considering joining a new group, I knew I really didn't want to work on these traditional technologies. I wanted to generate new ideas and I felt that these technologies were mature, and that any new work (for me) would be mainly incremental.

Centera was another story. Centera was not a block device, nor was it a file device. I was intrigued to learn that it was impossible to store content on a Centera without also storing a description of that content. What's more, these two pieces of information were literally thrown at a Centera. There were no instructions on where to physically or logically place them.

The application would subsequently read the content after receiving a claim check (think valet parking). Figure 18 depicts how Centera returns a content address anytime data is placed on the system.

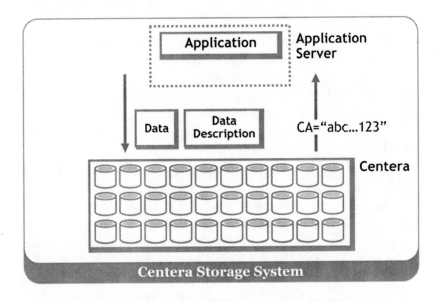

Figure 18. Centera accepts data descriptions and issues a content address.

For me, this concept was completely foreign. I was captivated, and I transferred to the Centera organization. My reasons for making this transfer were in line with my career strategy:

1. It was an adjacent technology. Surely my experience in storage technologies would be helpful to this new group, and thus grow my influence.

2. I would be learning a brand new technology: content addressing.
3. It was a virgin technology. No other company was doing anything remotely similar.
4. The possibilities for innovation seemed endless.

Motives 2 through 4 are my version of chasing the light bulb.

I had no idea how the Centera system was built, and I had built a storage system myself (CLARiiON). Centera was so different that I couldn't even imagine how it came together. I knew I would need to join the group and spend a good deal of time familiarizing myself with the technology. The possibility of learning new paradigms is a key draw for an innovative employee.

Centera was a virgin technology. It was so new, in fact, that there was no way to hook it up to an application server. Application servers knew how to talk to block storage systems, and they knew how to talk file storage systems, but they certainly didn't know anything about content addresses. I was even more intrigued with how Centera worked.

The possibilities for innovation were almost limitless and, with fifteen years of storage experience under my belt, I had influence with many spheres of expertise that might be joined with Centera, as highlighted in figure 19.

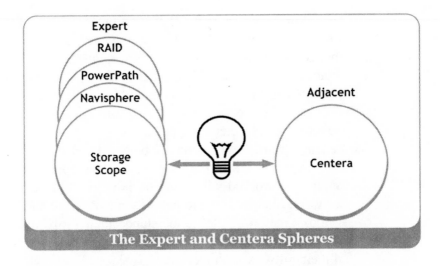

Figure 19. Multiple expert spheres could be combined with Centera.

Chasing the light bulb occurred because I was able to learn interesting new technologies, solve new customer problems (it was a virgin market), and visualize a large number of permutations or product possibilities.

My transfer occurred in April 2003. After my years in arm's-length research, I could hardly wait to return to the trenches. I would not be on the sidelines suggesting ideas; I would be working shoulder to shoulder with the developers. I would be productive and innovative, my two favorite things. In order to grow my influence in the Centera organization, I repeated the same steps I had used throughout my career. These steps, echoed in the chapters in this first section of the book, involved:

1. Getting It Done (early). My boss asked me to spend the entire summer understanding the internals of Centera. By mid-summer, I had completed a code

      review of the entire system, created presentations of how Centera worked, and recommended a set of changes to improve quality and performance.

2. Illuminating that First Idea. After studying Centera I presented my idea for a content-addressable router. The idea, of course, was based on an adjacent technology and a customer need.

3. Leading from the Trenches. I built a level of trust and support with the software developers in Belgium. I worked with them on how to build their software. I helped them to patent some of their ideas. I took the time to understand their software architecture and wrote a tool to highlight violations of their software architecture.

4. Overcoming the Innovator's Dilemma. I chose to re-architect improvements to the system that they had built.

5. Choosing to Stay or Go. I chose to stay with this technology and innovate via adjacent technologies.

6. Navigating Visibility. While in the Centera organization, I had strong horizontal visibility and virtually no executive visibility. My vertical visibility beyond my vice-president was negligible. I was left alone to innovate and deliver.

7. Leaving the Trenches. I decided to work with the developers who are designing the next generation Centera products. I've stayed close to the builders.

The move to the Centera organization started the most innovative phase of my career to date. The product has generated an enormous amount of revenue for EMC and I'm proud of my contribution to EMC's bottom line.

Influence: Chasing the Light Bulb

The best news of all (for me) is that I still see no end to the possibilities for innovation with object-based storage systems. I wrote a master's thesis on the topic. I've published two papers about the technology; one has been accepted for presentation at an industry conference. I've run internal coding challenges to help EMC employees learn the technology, and I have initiated an external coding challenge to educate the worldwide academic and business communities on the benefits of object-based storage.

My Centera experience has been so positive that I've decided to dedicate the upcoming section on innovation to Centera ideas arrived at using Venn diagram innovation.

In twenty years, I have changed from a college student who simply wanted to be productive, to an innovator who has influenced the storage industry. During this time, I chose to remain anonymous within the corporate structure of both of the large companies for which I worked. In doing so, I missed out on a good deal of recognition. Recognition, however, isn't all it's cracked up to be. Anonymity gave me the freedom to get it done, and it allowed me to live my life.

Live my life. As I finish this section on building influence, I'll start the one on innovation by describing the keys to inspiration. When I've been struggling for days on a tough problem with no apparent solution, there's an easy answer that's a car ride away. What's the best way to solve a problem?

Forget about it.

SECTION II: INNOVATION

10. Forget About It

It was the end of my senior year in college. I was writing software in my cubicle when my phone rang. It was my roommate, Murph.

"The guys in apartment J just challenged us to a wiffle ball game," Murph said.

"The J Foundation? They're challenging the Dream Team? Seriously?" I asked.

"They think you're too scared to show up," he said.

"See you in ten minutes," was my curt reply.

I hung up the phone and shouted over the wall to my boss, "I've got to run back to campus, see you tomorrow!" And out the door I went.

Life was easier as a co-op student getting paid by the hour, that's for sure. I enjoyed my work, but when it came to wiffle ball, well, I just liked that better.

Hanging out with my friends on campus meant a lot, much more than the $10 an hour I was making at Data General. Throughout the apartment complex where I lived were pairs of wiffle ball teammates that would talk trash to each other all week long. It was a great time. Thoughts of RAID algorithms were left far behind when I took to the wiffle ball field.

I share this story to highlight a philosophy I've stuck with for over twenty years: Work to live (as opposed to live to work). People are impressed with the number of patents I've generated, as well as the revenue my products have yielded. I'm here to say there's a little-known fact that is even more impressive.

I have left work at 5 p.m. for my entire career.

Anyone familiar with the high-tech industry will tell you this is no small feat. The pressure to stay late and stay often is ever-present.

I love my job, and I love the creative work I do, but to be quite honest, I would rather be playing wiffle ball. Granted, the Dream Team has been broken up for years and we've gone our separate ways, but when 5 p.m. rolls around, there's really no choice between staying at work or doing something else from my "want to" list:

- My wife is one of the most fun-loving, kind, and social people you will ever meet. Everyone wants to hang out with her; I'm married to her. She's the main reason I look forward to going home.
- My daughter plays middle hitter on her volleyball team. Watching her spike the ball is a fearsome thing. I love watching her games.
- My son plays catcher for the town baseball team. He can hit the long ball. My ears hurt just thinking about the sound a fastball makes when it hits his aluminum bat. I bring a bag of sunflower seeds to every game. Eat, spit, be happy.
- My dog, Boomer, is a 100% golden retriever. He fetches the paper from the end of our driveway each morning. When I get home, he assumes I've come to hit ground balls to him.
- My neighborhood softball team, the Winchester Bandits, moves me around the infield. Sometimes I play shortstop, other times I'm at first. We play a special brand of softball known as "Bandit ball," where age occasionally triumphs over quality.
- The local Boy Scout troop with which my son is involved often asks me to go on camping trips with

them. One summer, I went with them to Philmont Scout Ranch in New Mexico. I don't know who had the better time, the scouts or me.

- I have a 31' slide-out trailer that we take camping. Often times, we'll camp at the State Campground in Salisbury, Massachusetts. I've camped cross-country with my family several times.
- My local church has built several children's façades for church plays with the youth. I've written and directed several plays. My office is full of cast photos and pictures of some of my favorite local young actors and actresses.
- I've got a pond right behind my house that's bigger than a hockey rink. On winter nights after work, I'll bring down a lantern and the kids and I will skate for hours. Hot chocolate is usually involved.
- I played basketball at lunch for nearly twenty years, now I've retired for a hoop in the driveway with a spotlight overhead.
- Right around the corner from my house is a YMCA. I'm there early every morning, Monday through Friday.
- I'm on the board of directors for my church. We recently purchased and renovated a historic building in downtown Worcester that we're using to run social service programs. I'm a counselor for the youth group as well, and enjoy hanging out with the kids in the program.
- I live an hour away from my high school, and I am on the planning committee for reunions. I often drive up there just to hang out. My high school basketball coach is still coaching twenty-five years later, and

the North Andover hoops program has the longest consecutive streak of tournament appearances in the state of Massachusetts.

- Fenway Park is worth leaving work early for. My company actually has a program where employees get into the park for free and collect plastic for recycling.
- I split at least a cord of wood by hand each year and burn it all winter long. Smashing a maul against frozen logs is particularly enjoyable at the end of the workday. My golden retriever repeatedly brings me a frozen tennis ball during this activity.
- I regularly plan family vacations to spots throughout the world. Ireland and Scotland were last year; the Mediterranean is on the radar. We work on a lot of scrapbooks and have a travel wall in our basement that's covered with photos of our various vacations.
- I have a lot of backpacking gear and take my son and dog to New Hampshire's White Mountains every chance I get.
- My wife's family owns a home on the Cape Cod Canal. This past year, we did a whale watch right off the point of the Cape (Provincetown). The Cape is reasonable driving distance from my office.

I would rather do any of these activities than build software. I clearly want to have a fulfilling work life, but I work mainly to fund my personal life. I want to minimize my work hours, maximize my dollars per hour, and fund the living of a full life.

I've made it a point during my career to keep this approach low-key (as in let's not ruin a good thing). Certainly my co-workers all notice that when 5 p.m. rolls around, I'm not in my office anymore. But they also know that my work has been completed early. I'm productive.

How does management feel about my work hours? In over twenty years of discussions with my managers, the issue has come up exactly once. In my very first performance review, my boss told me that I was doing a super job, and that I was highly productive. He then went on to mention that I may find myself ineligible to receive the additional bonuses handed out to employees that put in longer hours.

For example, one of my co-workers regularly stayed at work until 7 or 8 p.m. every night. My company recognized him with a quarterly bonus on the order of $500 to $1,000.

I decided right then and there that these bonuses were not for me. My boss was correct to tell me about this potential missed opportunity, as well as to tell me that my working style might leave me on the outside looking in when it came to some extra spending money.

But this approach violates my philosophy: maximize the amount of dollars earned per hour, and maximize the amount of hours spent outside of work. A quarterly bonus of $1,000 at 10 hours extra per week works out to about $5 per hour, after taxes.

So, do I play wiffle ball, or do I work for $5 an hour?

I made the same choice every time: Work to live.

I wasn't doing it for the sake of innovation. Looking back now, however, I can see the passion for all things non-work gave me the emotional, mental, and physical health that fueled my creative drive. I'd try and solve tough problems all day long, and then I'd leave.

And I'd forget about them.

Distancing myself from the tough problems allowed me to think clearly and return to work each day with a fresh set of eyes.

My subconscious tends to want to solve work problems around the clock. This is why my first waking moments are often filled with thoughts of work. This makes it all the more important for me to make certain I push myself to have fun.

I can't stress this practice enough, which is why I have dedicated a whole chapter describing and justifying the approach. My track record is proof positive that innovating with influence can be accomplished by way of a distinct and unwavering separation between work and life.

I no longer have to keep this approach under wraps for fear of being asked to put in more hours. Most companies recognize the value of the work-life balance, and know that it is a crucial job satisfaction criterion for many employees. However, leaving early is a choice in the same way that pursuing innovation is a choice. Companies are certainly not going to force anyone to leave early!

Do I do any work at all once I get home? Of course. It's nearly impossible to fully disengage, given the level of connectivity available from home. Most of this work falls into the category of communication, whether it be e-mail, social media, or writing blog posts. There's not a lot of innovative heavy lifting that I do at home. I've got other plans.

So I did leave my cubicle in May 1987 and I drove back to campus. I parked my car and walked over to Murphy Memorial Stadium in front of our apartment. I took my spot in left field, Murph started throwing his variety of off-speed pitches with names such as The Squiggler and Knuckles Nuclear. The taunting of the members of the J Foundation began. We beat them.

We beat everybody that spring. As graduation approached, the Dream Team went on a winning streak that carried us to the championship game for the entire apartment complex. And when the last pitch was thrown and the Dream

Team had recorded the final out, Murph disappeared into the apartment complex, ran up the stairs, and came down with a bottle of champagne. He uncorked it and proceeded to dump it over my head.

I don't remember all of the details about that day. I don't remember if my eyes stung as the champagne dripped down my face.

I know for sure there was one thing that I wasn't thinking about.

I wasn't thinking about work.

11. Venn Diagram Innovation

I've described how nearly all of the ideas I've generated have sprung from the three spheres of innovation. This practice was not something that I consciously followed throughout my career. In hindsight, however, I can see that my innovative activity was most often the result of an intersection of customer problems, my own expertise, and adjacent technologies. This became particularly apparent to me as I looked back on my experience working in the Centera organization.

When I joined EMC's Centera organization in 2003, I took on the responsibility of getting to know the software written by the Belgian engineers and recommending improvements to the existing product. Within several months, however, I was given a new task: Create a "sandbox" for quick prototyping of new ideas. The Centera technology, known as content addressable storage (CAS), was a new technology full of potential. If my team could create an agile environment for building (and demonstrating) new ideas, it was EMC's hope that we could propose solutions to customer problems more quickly.

Although it doesn't matter whether the customer is internal or external, in this particular case, the customer was internal: The Centera development organization. We wanted a framework for testing and building new CAS solutions. My area of expertise, by that time, was Centera. These two spheres (expert and customer) represent the starting point for innovation, as demonstrated in figure 20.

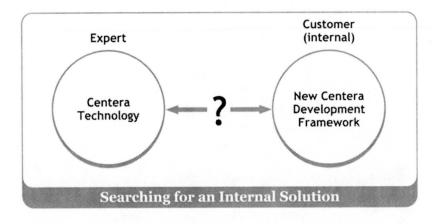

Figure 20. Two spheres (expert and customer) are often the starting point.

If a customer, for example, asked our engineers to propose a method to aggregate Centera systems, my group accepted the challenge to experiment quickly with solutions in this new framework. If customers asked for a solution to search and index the content stored on a Centera, the framework should provide the environment in which to test different ways of building such a product. For any new feature that might be built, our group needed a sandbox in which to play.

Given two known spheres, all that remained for innovation was to find an adjacent technology. In my case, I already had a variety of technologies in my armory, and one of them was PowerPath. I had worked with the team of engineers in Cork, Ireland, on the development of the data migration software, so I knew the software architecture created by the PowerPath team allowed for new features to be quickly added into a stack of features, as depicted in figure 21.

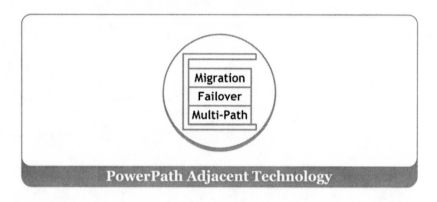

Figure 21. PowerPath allows easy insertion of new features.

In figure 21, application write operations flow into the "clamp" (the C-shaped structure), down through the features, and out of the bottom of the clamp to a disk. The migration feature managed migration operations, the failover feature managed the routing of application operations in the face of failures, and the multi-path feature managed the performance load balancing over several different paths.

Could this architecture be deployed for operations flowing to and from a Centera storage system?

I liked this approach. By borrowing an idea from an adjacent technology, an idea was born. This idea would be "PowerPath-like"; Centera requests would be run through a layered stack of features and decisions would be made on how to handle or filter these requests, as depicted in figure 22. All that was needed was a name. I decided to call this idea the CAS Router.

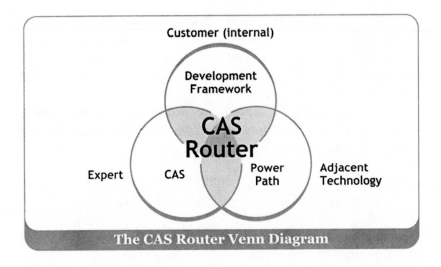

Figure 22. CAS Router idea was also the result of Venn Diagram Innovation.

This concept of intercepting, processing, and forwarding CAS requests was new and valuable. Over time, external and other internal customers expressed requirements that could be solved by a CAS Router. They expressed a desire to migrate content between systems, and they expressed a desire to aggregate multiple systems. The CAS Router concept was moved into the development organization to be further developed.

This was my first innovation in the Centera organization. The second innovation was also pulled from another sphere with which I had developed familiarity.

Many Centera customers were sharing their Centera systems among multiple internal organizations. For example, some customers were allowing their marketing employees to store finalized presentations on Centera, while simultaneously allowing customer support teams to store field documents and white papers on the same Centera box. Eventually, these customers expressed a desire to be able to issue separate bills to each organization based on the amount of data being stored by each different group. For example, a Centera system administrator might wish to charge a certain amount per organization in what is commonly referred to as a chargeback.

Centera didn't have any such product that could accomplish this task. It was an opportunity to innovate, starting with the Venn diagram depicted in figure 23.

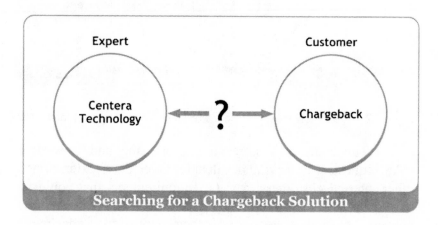

Figure 23. A Chargeback solution required an adjacent technology.

The adjacent sphere, in this case, was a technology I had used before: StorageScope. Storage Scope was a billing and reporting tool that performed hardware chargeback on the physical allocation of storage resources to different organizations. This time, the customer requirement wasn't for the abiility to perform chargebacks on hardware but on content.

Working with a team of Centera engineers, we summarized some of the logic behind the StorageScope product and translated this logic into a set of requirements that were applicable to Centera. The key, it turned out, was the data description that Centera always stores along with the content. This data description, often referred to as *meta data*, can contain information about which organization wrote the data, which could reasonably be extrapolated to calculate which organizations generated which pieces of content. Our idea and strategy were soon documented and a product was proposed.

In 2006, Centera Seek was released to the market. Combining relevant qualities from the three spheres on the Venn diagram (see figure 24), this innovative product was one of the first of its kind in the industry. Centera Seek was built as an appliance outside of a Centera; future plans would allow for this functionality to move inside the Centera system.

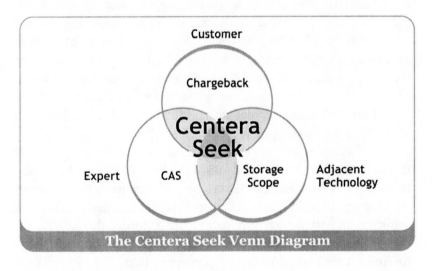

Figure 24. Venn diagram for Centera Seek.

Not only have I participated personally in this type of innovation that incorporates expertise, adjacent technology, and a customer requirement, but I have also seen this pattern practiced repeatedly across my corporation. Each of the approximately forty companies EMC has acquired in the past decade brings along with it a new (to EMC) adjacent technology. There are potentially hundreds of new products to be dreamed up by brainstorming between adjacent technologies. Many of these ideas will map directly to customers' expressed and as yet unrealized needs.

For example, data security is an extremely important customer requirement. It's one of the reasons why EMC acquired RSA, the organization behind those little remote-login key fobs. When it comes to security, RSA is a thought leader and a product leader.

Given the fact that SANs contain storage devices that are essentially shared among various application servers, many customers are concerned that a hacker can snoop the data on the SAN and steal what is being written. These customers expressed a strong desire to encrypt the data flowing between their application server and their data storage devices. Encryption would guarantee that hackers snooping on the SAN would be unable to interpret stolen information (unless they had also stolen the decryption keys).

When RSA experts needed to find an adjacent technology that transferred information onto a SAN, they looked to PowerPath. PowerPath's software stack allows developers to add new features that intercept the flow of information between an application and a storage device.

PowerPath developers worked with their peers at RSA to integrate *encryption key services* into the PowerPath framework. This approach enabled customers to add a secure key server into their environment, which, in turn, allowed PowerPath to encrypt information on its way to a storage system and decrypt the same information on the way back, as depicted in figure 25. This new product (named PowerPath Encryption w/RSA) was released by EMC in 2008.

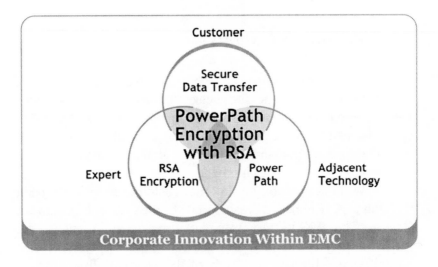

Figure 25. A solution formed from acquired companies.

This example highlights the opportunities that innovators can encounter at large companies. It's often said that large companies can't provide the innovative experiences available at start-ups or small companies. I don't agree. Smaller companies don't have as great a depth of technologies within their ranks, and they don't have the number of experts that come with each one. Innovative collaboration at large companies has much more potential to occur and succeed.

It's also my assertion that, given the right culture and the right corporate talent, innovation at large companies can be much more fun. That's right, I used the word fun. I frequently describe the work that goes on at EMC as an information playground.

And speaking of fun, there's nothing more fun than innovating with the third sphere in the Venn diagram: The customer.

12. Customer Site Innovation

My favorite way to start the innovative process is to visit the customers using the products, technologies, and services I've worked on. Venn diagram innovation always takes customer need into account and, when innovators learn about customer needs firsthand (preferably at the customer site), it accelerates the urgency to innovate and deliver.

Without a doubt, my favorite customer to visit has been the John F. Kennedy Presidential Library and Museum in Boston. The JFK Library is undertaking an ambitious digital archiving project in which they are attempting to preserve, with digital means, literally hundreds of thousands of JFK's papers and photos (as well as audio and video clips) related to his presidency. These digital assets will eventually be available to researchers worldwide via Internet-based presentation software.

I showed up at the JFK Library in early 2008 in order to understand how the system the archivists were using had been deployed. I also scheduled follow-up visits to understand the process being employed. I was trying to get a better understanding of the archivists' requirements.

Figure 26 represents a simplified diagram describing the process and products I observed at the JFK Library.

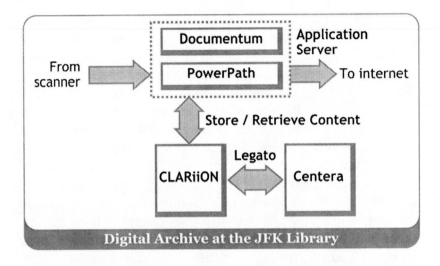

Figure 26. The archive at the JFK Library contains multiple products.

JFK archivists are overseeing the scanning process of JFK's legacy by using EMC Documentum® software. Documentum handles all aspects of the archiving workflow: It interfaces with the scanner, allows the archivist to add additional information (meta data) about the content, and will enable (once the digital archive is open to the public) access to the archive over the Internet.

Documentum stores the data and the meta data directly to a CLARiiON system. PowerPath is used to provide load-balancing and failure re-routing over several different paths to the storage. The CLARiiON provides the initial high-speed and robust storage of the information. The Centera is used as the "deep archive" to store hundreds of thousands of these digital artifacts. EMC Legato software transparently moves the content between CLARiiON and Centera as required.

While the archivists were explaining the configuration and their process for using the equipment, they handed me a document they were about to scan. In my hands I held a paper from the desk of President Kennedy. It was at that moment that I realized the magnitude and importance of the project they were undertaking. These artifacts were owned by the citizens of the United States, but traditionally they were only available to dedicated groups of researchers. The digital archiving project will eventually open up access to large numbers of U.S. citizens (not to mention interested citizens of other countries!).

I myself am a customer of this solution, to some degree.

I understood clearly the technology that was in place at the JFK Library. I had a lot to learn, however, when it came to the digitizing process the archivists were using. It turns out that there are industry standard guidelines that archivists must follow when preserving content to a digital archive. For example, consider the following meta data that also must be generated when JFK's assets (known in the archiving industry as *data objects*) are stored into the archive:

- *Representation information*: additional information describing how to interpret the data object. Is it a scanned image? Is it an audio clip understood by a specific media player? Is it a video file in a particular DVD format?

- *Reference information*: an identifier used to refer to the content. For example, the JFK Library has boxes of folders containing JFK's assets; these folders have a specific naming scheme that is being recorded as part of the reference information (e.g., JFKPOF-001-003).

- *Provenance information*: represents an annotated history of the data object (e.g., the name of the person who originally generated the content, the initial archivist, and information about the migration of content to a new location).

- *Context information*: gives additional context about the data object (e.g., why it was created and/or how it relates to other data objects).

- *Fixity information*: contains authentication and authenticity keys that are necessary to confirm that the content has not been altered.

Given these standards, the archivists at the JFK Library use Documentum to enter and store this extra information. It can be a tedious process but well worth the effort because it ensures the long-term preservation of America's cultural heritage. I watched as the archivists entered this information into the system.

When it came time for the archivists to enter the representation information into the system, they typed a very detailed description of the scanning equipment and process they were using. They entered the make and model number of the scanner. They entered the name and version of the Documentum software that integrated with the scanner. They entered the format type of the scanned image (e.g., 600 DPI TIFF files). It was a thorough and accurate catalog of the environment.

Something about the process worried me. I wondered whether the software of the future would be able to interpret the data being archived in the present! One hundred years from now, when an archivist wishes to look at one of these documents and reads "600 DPI TIFF," will TIFF still be a supported format? Will Documentum still be available? If TIFF is still supported and Documentum is still available, will it still be able to interpret information generated in formats written decades earlier?

This problem is well known in the storage industry and, in some circles, has been called the "100-year problem." The archivists at the JFK Library were being as thorough as as they could possibly be, given the tools they were using. It appeared to me, however, that there had to be a better way. To put this in an innovative context, I was looking at two thirds of the Venn diagram puzzle depicted in figure 27.

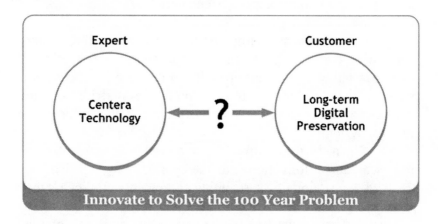

Figure 27. Venn diagram innovation to solve the 100-year problem.

What does an innovator do next? An innovator finds an adjacent technology. In this case, I did not actively commit myself to solving this problem; it was more of an observation I had made at a customer site. I put the observation on a back burner in my mind. Several weeks later, I had an experience with another adjacent technology within a company in which EMC holds a majority ownership: VMware.

VMware creates many different products and services. One of them allows a customer to capture its entire application environment (both the operating system and the applications) into a file. This file can then be opened by another VMware application (VMware Player). VMware Player treats the file as though it were an actual computer. A customer pushes the "on" button, VMware Player boots up the file and the customer can then log in and run his or her applications from the VMware Player screen.

This is very cool technology. A computing environment can be saved as a file.

Cool technology, of course, gets me thinking.

Can I archive a VMware file for 100 years? Of course I can.

Would a VMware Player user of the future be able to push the on button for this file and boot up an image that is 100 years old?

I didn't know, but I sketched out how the process might work. This sketch, depicted in figure 28, shows how archiving a VMware file to a Centera could be handled.

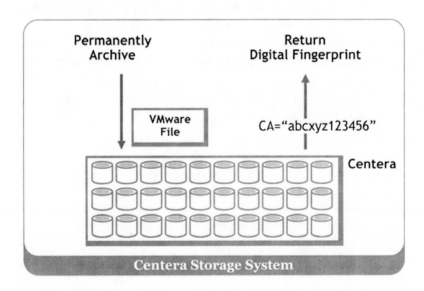

Figure 28. Theoretical process flow using VMware and Centera.

This process results in a unique digital fingerprint ("abcxyz123456") that will forever map to the computing environment being archived onto the Centera.

Consider it this way. Assume that the computing environment is exactly equivalent to the one being used by the archivists at the JFK Library. The operating system is a specific version of Microsoft® Windows®. This version of Windows comes with a TIFF reader that can interpret the TIFF format. Installed atop Windows is a specific version of Documentum that allows access to the meta data stored along with the TIFF image. VMware can capture all of this software and store it as a file. An archivist can store this file and record the unique digital fingerprint (known as a content address or CA in Centera-speak). The archivist can call this particular content address a "VM-CA."

The use of this technique would allow an archivist to use a much different technique when storing representation information to an archive. Instead of typing a description of the computing environment, the archivist can now directly point to the actual computing environment itself by associating the archived content with its VM-CA. Figure 29 depicts a Centera archive containing a document with associated reference information (RI) that points directly to the VMWARE image.

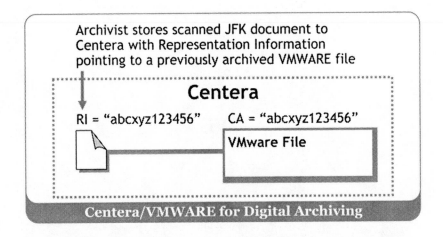

Figure 29. A document on Centera is associated with a VMware image.

If this idea is taken to its logical conclusion, an archivist wishing to view this document 100 years from now would simply boot up the computer used to generate the content 100 years earlier.

Are there holes in this idea? I would assume so, because the devil is always in the details.

Will this idea be shipped as a product? That would depend on my level of influence. However, my company is already on board with the research, so I am optimistic.

The reason I described this particular idea was to demonstrate how some of the most powerful ideas can sprout from direct contact and collaboration with the customer. Since every product, actual and potential, needs a name, I called this innovation Centera and VMware for Digital Archiving (CVDA). The Venn diagram for this innovation is provided in Figure 30.

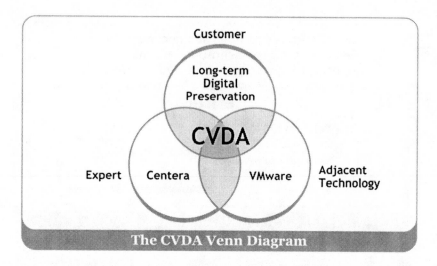

Figure 30. Venn diagram for Centera and VMware for Digital Archiving.

Customer innovation, in this context, is the most important type of innovation. It addresses directly a problem from the customer sphere.

Is it advisable to innovate without considering any specific customer problem? I believe the answer to this question is yes. I have done this many times in my career. I call it blue sky innovation and it's characterized by idea exchange between adjacent technologies. Something important typically happens during the blue sky innovation process.

The customer inevitably shows up.

13. Blue Sky Innovation

One afternoon in 2005, I was getting a haircut at work. Cynthia is a hair stylist who maintains an office in the EMC facilities in Hopkinton. She has her own little hair salon set-up, great prices, and fast service. She's been giving haircuts at EMC for most of the decade and one wall of her salon includes a window that looks out on a pit of engineers' cubicles. How did I know they were engineers? Because they looked nerdy.

Most of the engineers (myself included) in my building worked for the Centera organization. The engineers I saw through her window, however, were unfamiliar to me. When Cynthia had finished cutting my hair, I strolled over to their cubicles and saw a sign at the entrance to their area. The sign read, "Grid Business Unit."

So this was the grid team. How cool. I didn't know the grid engineers were in the same building as Centera.

A *grid* is a network of computers linked together to run jobs (or tasks) on demand. Whenever a customer wanted to run a job, the customer could essentially "rent" a portion of a set of computers to run the job. It didn't matter where that job would run. The grid software would find some free computers, assign the job to those computers, and off they would go.

Ever since the creation of the Grid Business Unit had been announced, I had wanted to learn more about this technology. More precisely, I wanted to know how it worked. How does a job get submitted? How does the software keep track of available resources? How does the job get sent to those resources? How does storage get hooked up to a grid?

The aspect that interested me most about grid technology was that it was *location-independent*. Whenever a job needed to run, there was no way or need to know where it would end up running. A simplistic diagram showing how "Job A" is assigned to idle computers 11, 12, 15, and 16 is depicted in figure 31.

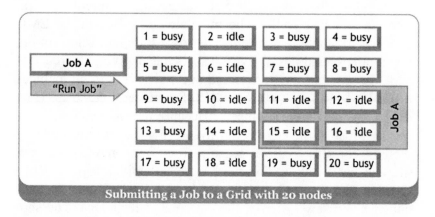

Figure 31. A simplistic diagram of a job submitted to a grid.

Sporting a fresh haircut and news about the presence of the grid team in the building, I went back to my desk and put my feet up for a few minutes and thought. I didn't have time to learn about grid technology at that particular moment because I was in the middle of a Centera project. During my pondering, though, it occurred to me that Centera was also a location-independent technology. When applications stored information to a Centera, they were unaware as to where the information would end up being stored physically. It didn't matter. Valet parking attendants don't tell people where their cars get parked; the Centera products don't tell applications where their information gets stored.

Customers use a claim check in order to get back their car from the valet parking attendant. Applications use a content address in order to get their information back from Centera.

Centera is location-independent storage.

Grid is location-independent computing.

There had to be an innovation opportunity in there somewhere.

I put the potential marriage between grid and Centera on the back burner. Grid computing was clearly an adjacent technology, even though I had no idea what customer problem it would solve.

Eventually, the opportunity arose for me to have a discussion with the chief technology officer of the grid business unit. I knew we'd hit it off when I told him that I thought we should get together and "blue sky" for a while and he said, "I've wanted to talk to the Centera group for a long time. There are a lot of similarities."

My own particular pattern of innovation always seems to involve three spheres, one of which always represents the customer's requirements. With blue sky innovation, the customer sphere is initially left out of the picture, as shown in figure 32.

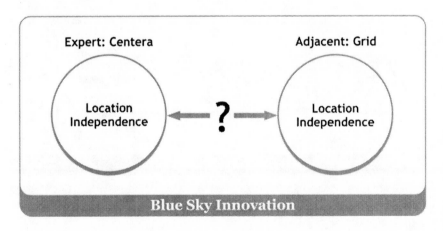

Figure 32. Blue sky innovation may not initially include the customer.

We met and discussed our respective group's technologies. I told him everything I knew about Centera; he told me everything he knew about grid.

I told him that every piece of information stored on Centera always has two characteristics:

1. It is stored with "extra information" (meta data).
2. The information and the meta data are represented by an identifier known as a content address (CA).

It was at this point that a light bulb went on in his head. I could see it in his eyes, actually.

"I talk to customers all the time," he said, "about taking the output of one grid job and using it as input into another. There are times when grid customers create a pipeline of grid jobs and pass the output of one into the input of the next." Dan drew a diagram for me, a version of which is presented in figure 33.

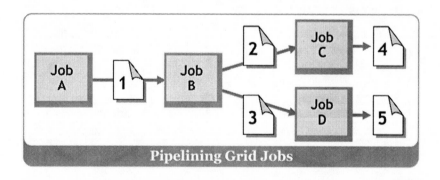

Figure 33. Pipelined grid jobs pass output from one job to the next.

"Often times our grid customers get to the end result and, after weeks of analysis, they want to return to a previous document, but they can't trace the lineage." By lineage, he was referring to the genealogy of the customer data. In figure 33, for example, document 4 is descended from documents 2 and 1, while document 5 is descended from documents 3 and 1.

He went on to explain that his current grid customers did not have the ability, for any given document, to backtrack to any of its descendants. Furthermore, they did not necessarily have a way to link a given document back to the job that created it. Customers wanted a graph of their data sets and their jobs, and they wanted the ability to use that graph to backtrack to a previous state.

This problem is not new to the storage industry. It is known as the *data provenance* problem.

Something pretty cool was happening. I had gone off to blue sky without a customer problem. My co-worker brought along grid expertise and a customer need: data provenance.

We had just found the adjacent technology to solve the data provenance problem, and that technology was Centera.

We combined two of Centera's unique features (meta data capture and content addressing) to build data lineage graphs of jobs, inputs, and outputs. Consider figure 34, which shows "job A" and "document 1" after being stored onto a Centera.

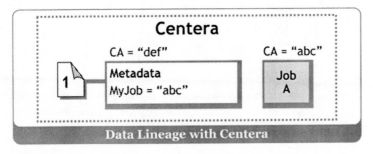

Figure 34. Identifying data lineage with Centera.

The idea focused on using Centera's meta data feature to point back to the job that created document 1. Job A was stored to Centera, which generated a content address of "abc." When document 1 was stored to Centera, it was also stored with meta data that pointed to the job that created it. Document 1, and its associated meta data, is represented with a content address of "def."

Now consider the Centera system after job B had run, as depicted in Figure 35 .

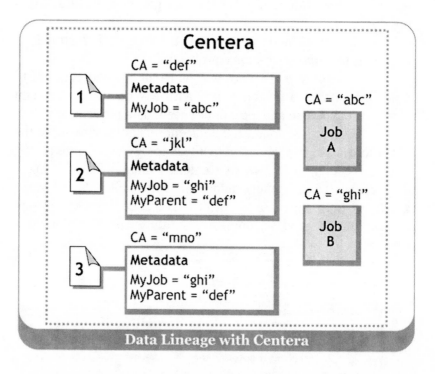

Figure 35. Centera supports increasingly complex data lineage.

Job B creates two new pieces of content (documents 2 and 3). When each of these documents were stored to Centera, they pointed back not only to the job that created them (job B, with a content address of "ghi"), but they also pointed to their common parent document, document 1 (represented by the content address "def").

This process is repeated each time a new grid job takes previous outputs, uses them as inputs, and generates new outputs. At the end of this process, customers now have a data lineage graph that allows them to backtrack to any ancestor and any ancestral job. We began brainstorming about a graphical display of this information, which would look like the depiction in figure 36.

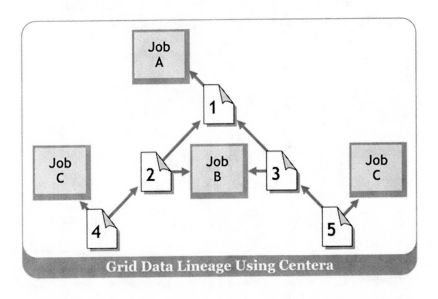

Figure 36. Lineage using Centera backtracks through multiple generations.

Interestingly enough, we had "blue-skyed" an innovative solution that went well beyond the grid market.

Imagine a company running analytic jobs in order to generate quarterly financial statements. What if they wanted to go back and fix something? What if one of the jobs that generated their data needed fixing? No problem; just backtrack to where the change needs to be made.

Imagine huge amounts of scientific data being processed and analyzed, which, in turn, generates more data to be processed and analyzed. Or imagine radiology scans that result in a false-positive diagnosis. Or imagine legal determination of royalty payouts when multiple pieces of copyrighted material are combined to generate a single document.

The possibilities are endless. Blue sky innovation works when the customer shows up, as depicted in figure 37.

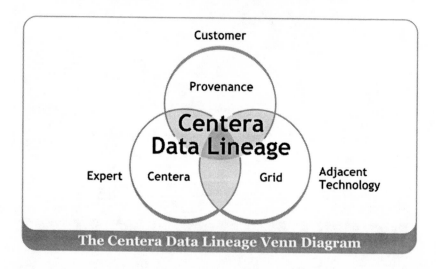

Figure 37. Venn diagram of a Centera data lineage solution for provenance.

At this point, we were just two guys in a room brainstorming. We had used the blue sky innovation process to come up with an idea that (we believed) should be instantly funded by our company and take over the world.

Of course, things don't always work out that way. Innovation must churn through the gears of influence in order to make it into customer hands.

The initiative to explore grid and Centera opportunities had simmered on the back burner until I found a spare moment to meet with one of my peers.

This particular idea was then moved off of the back burner.

I decided to turn up the innovative heat myself.

14. Innovative Heat

In my office I have a piece of paper with two vertical lines separating the paper into thirds. On this paper, I write down everything that I either have to do or want to do.

In the left-hand column, I write down my commitments to my employer.

In the middle column, I write down the things I really, really want to work on.

In the right-hand column, I write down any innovative ideas I might like to pursue in the future.

In chapter 13, I described how a blue sky innovation process had generated an idea for a Centera and data lineage solution. The idea to collaborate with the grid business unit had been on my personal back burner ever since I saw their cubicles through Cynthia's hair salon window. I decided to turn up the innovative heat and move the entry from the right-hand column to the middle. I really, really wanted to pursue the idea. Not only did it directly solve an important customer problem, but it also represented a solution that few other companies could offer (given the uniqueness of the Centera product).

I had to find some time to work on it. However, my manager, his manager, and everybody else on up the line was expecting me to deliver something else. That something else would be the product that I am currently building. Put another way, that something else would be my job.

When it comes to what I'm supposed to be working on, I have to take my own advice. I get it done.

However, I also want to work on all the other innovative items on my list. In order to do this as well, I need to take my own advice again.

I need to get it done early.

It is easy to say, but it is so hard to do.

That's why I always keep that paper in front of me, to remind me to turn up the heat. I always have those spare moments during the day where I become free for a few minutes. I also have those spare moments during the day when it's time to take a break. When I have my ideas sitting right in front of me, the wheels seem to start turning all by themselves. I can turn up the innovative heat a bit higher every time I see that list.

Figure 38 shows the three columns of innovation that are sitting on my desk as of right now.

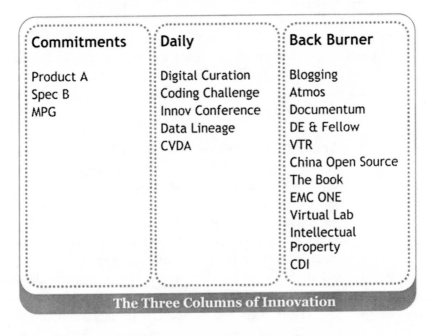

Commitments	Daily	Back Burner
Product A	Digital Curation	Blogging
Spec B	Coding Challenge	Atmos
MPG	Innov Conference	Documentum
	Data Lineage	DE & Fellow
	CVDA	VTR
		China Open Source
		The Book
		EMC ONE
		Virtual Lab
		Intellectual Property
		CDI

The Three Columns of Innovation

Figure 38. My list of commitments, innovation, and personal projects.

Every single item on this list represents innovation. All of them. That's my goal. While the items on the left-hand side may not seem like innovation (due to the daily grind of building software for the storage industry), they represent past innovation that is evolving into product. I only want to work on the projects that are highly innovative. That's the type of work my management gives me, because they know I can get it done.

So what does the shorthand on my current list mean?

Commitments

My group is building a storage product (product A). It is highly innovative and I'm very motivated to see it succeed. I've been working on it for over two years, and the team is nearing code completion. This item is on the top of my list, followed closely by two others. While I enjoy the overall work, there are hours and hours of time spent on the normal and regular tasks associated with building software:

- Project A: my work on this project has mainly been architectural and design-oriented. There are dozens of people in the trenches cranking out the software to realize the design. I own the system specification document, which describes the product we are building. If anybody in the organization needs that specification updated, they come through me. Lately, it's been quiet on this front, but it's the highest priority item on my plate.
- Spec B: I own the generation of an architectural description of our follow-on product (project B). I'm working with a team of architects on a blueprint for our next generation software. This blueprint will guide the trenches on how to build what comes next.

Creating this description takes hours of my time. Some days, I type from the moment that I get in until quitting time.

- MPG: I work in the multi-protocol platform group (MPG). Project A and project B have strong ties to other programs and products within MPG and I spend hours in meetings with trench developers making sure that the product set we deliver provides customer value efficiently and effectively.

This column represents the daily grind. There's not a lot of active innovation occurring daily. The innovative ideas that launched my group and my products happened over two years ago. I'm using my influence to deliver the innovation into customer hands. In my business, this activity can sometimes take years.

Daily Innovation

This column represents items that have moved off of the back burner. At some point in the past, I had an innovative thought or concept and I threw it onto the back burner list. These items, for one reason or another, have increased in importance in my mind and therefore I've decided to turn up the innovative heat and pursue them with intention.

I use the term "daily innovation" because I believe, in order to make progress on these ideas, I need to aim for spending thirty to sixty minutes per day on at least one of them. If I'm not able to get anything done on the daily innovation items, it's because my commitments are taking priority. However, if I can get my commitments done early, then I can usually squeeze in some work on the daily innovation items.

Having this list right next to my desk helps to keep these thoughts alive and well at all times.

- *Digital Curation*: I submitted a research paper to the Digital Curation Conference in Edinburgh, Scotland. It was accepted and will be published. A co-worker of mine presented the paper. I'm promoting the use of content addressing to digital curators, hoping to raise awareness and promote research using products like Centera.

- *Coding challenge*: I recently ran a coding challenge across my business unit (MPG). EMC has partnered with other vendors in my industry to create a new technology known as *extensible access method* (XAM). I thought it would be a good idea to promote internal development of XAM applications via a contest. It worked. Now I'm trying to promote a worldwide external coding challenge using XAM technology.

- *Innovation conference*: EMC holds a yearly innovation conference in October. I participated in the inaugural event and enjoyed it to the point that I called the conference organizer and said, "I want to help." We meet for one hour every week. The conference has become a critical part of EMC's Innovative DNA.

- *Data lineage*: The Centera data lineage idea was proposed during a contest at the 2007 EMC Innovation Conference, and our idea came in third place. EMC assigned an R&D team in China to work on the idea with us, and we built a prototype within six months. It was then shown to customers. Work is ongoing to turn this idea into a product.

- *CVDA*: Centera-VMware digital archiving was also proposed as an idea at EMC's 2008 Innovation Conference, and came in second place out of 984 worldwide entries. I will be working with another team to build a proof of concept and, I hope, ultimately productize the idea.
- *Industry news*: I always keep up on the happenings in the storage and information industry. My most common source of information these days is the bloggers who write about this field. I contribute my own thoughts as well.

All of these ideas are active. They've moved off the back burner and require a meeting every once in a while. They often also require a bit of writing or some slide creation or modification for presentations. They sometimes get ignored on occasion because of my "real" commitments, but I frequently scan this list when I have a spare moment, and I roll the ball forward as I see fit.

Back Burner

The back burner column represents my own personal holding tank of ideas. They are the fun part of my job; I often think about them as I'm driving back and forth to work. These ideas were born from blue sky thinking, customer interactions, and conversations with experts in adjacent technologies.

- *Blogging*: I maintain my own personal, external blog. I maintain an internal one as well. I post many of my ideas on these blogs in order to stimulate dialogue. This usually takes me less than thirty minutes. Sometimes I'll do two or three posts in a week, sometimes none. I spend five to ten minutes daily on EMC ONE, an internal employee collaboration platform.

- *Atmos*: EMC announced a global storage system known as Atmos in 2008. It's an adjacent technology that really interests me. I learned about it and I've written several external blogs about the product. I don't know where my interest will lead me, but it sounds like an opportunity for blue sky innovation.

- *Documentum*: I still visit the JFK library when I get a chance. I'd like to learn more about the Documentum technology. I'm particularly interested in adding workflow interfaces to Documentum that are specific to digital archivists. This work would help the team at the JFK Library. I've sent a few e-mails to the Documentum experts; I hope to meet with them soon.

- *DE & Fellow Program*: EMC runs a nomination process called the Distinguished Engineers and Fellows program. I was awarded the title of Distinguished Engineer (DE) recently and some of my co-workers from human resources have asked for ideas on how to manage this community. I'd like to help and have already submitted the idea that each DE/Fellow be assigned to a customer to stimulate customer-based innovation.

- *VTR*: EMC Visual Talk Radio, as far as I know, is a first in the information industry. It's a live internal radio show that occurs every three weeks. Guests speak on a variety of topics. Listeners can call or text live questions to the host and guests. The entire show is recorded for subsequent listening. Radio listeners can watch the visuals on their laptops. I've been a guest, a co-host, and am involved in designing the programming for any future radio shows on the topic of innovation.

- *China open source*: my co-workers in China have been developing software for the Centera data lineage idea. I'd like to give them Centera source code and allow them to collaborate on its development. I would need to design some open-source governance rules and manage the logistics for code sharing (the China team is not part of my business unit).
- *The book*: the idea for this book was born while I was listening to EMC Visual Talk Radio at lunch one day. The guests were suggesting that the development of an employee's personal brand (e.g., I'm an innovator with influence) intersects and promotes a company's employment brand (e.g., EMC is an innovative place to work).
- *EMC ONE*: Our internal social media platform is known as EMC ONE, and I use this platform regularly. I strongly feel that EMC ONE (or something like it) should be adopted by employees throughout the world. Other companies use technologies to connect virtually with each other. I'm interested in helping to make this happen as well.
- *Virtual lab*: I was assigned to a team of technologists who met with EMC's head legal counsel, Paul Dacier. Paul pointed out that power rates for electricity vary throughout the world. The cost of powering labs here in Massachusetts is enormous. He wondered if there was any way to build a virtual

lab that was nimble enough to move to wherever power costs were the lowest. He gave this assignment to our team.

- *Intellectual property*: EMC has a common portal for submitting patent ideas (also known as invention disclosures). I regularly take ideas (many of them come from the back burner list) and submit an invention disclosure form. I meet with patent attorneys regularly to file patents. Being that the inventions always involve adjacent technologies, I rarely submit ideas as a sole inventor.

- *CDI*: Customer downloadable innovation (CDI) is another idea I'd like to formalize. When the China R&D team built a Centera data lineage proof of concept product, they built it as a VMware virtual appliance. This virtual appliance is a file. We brought this file to a customer demo and showed it to them. They gave us their business cards to hear more about the idea. I want to go further than this. I want to create a library of VMware virtual appliances that makes EMC research available to EMC's customers. These customers would be able to download and play with our latest thinking, and then collaborate with us on the directions that we're taking.

This three-column piece of paper represents my current life of innovation. The three columns make it a pleasure to drive to work each day. I often use pyramids to highlight two important aspects of these three columns: time spent and number of ideas, as represented in figure 39.

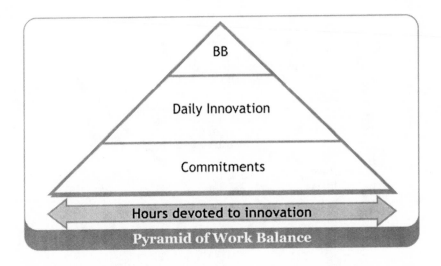

Figure 39. A different view of the three columns of innovation.

The hours spent on my corporate commitments should far exceed the hours I spend on daily innovation. Why? First of all, it's a matter of integrity. I should be working on the items that I've promised to deliver. Second, as I've mentioned many times, delivering on my commitments increases my influence. Influence is more important than innovation.

The second pyramid I associate with these three columns is inverted. It represents the number of ideas that exist in each column. It's a top-heavy picture, as shown in figure 40.

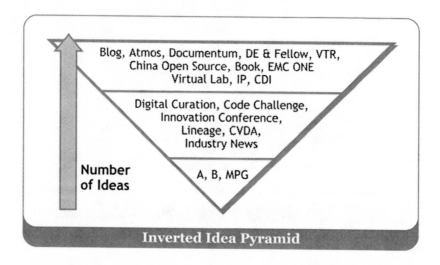

Figure 40. A visualization of more back burner ideas than commitments.

Visualizing the three columns as an inverted pyramid can actually be disheartening. One could look at the number of ideas and express fear that it's impossible for all of them to trickle down to the level of commitment. In other words, there's no way that all of these ideas could ever be realized by one individual, no matter how influential that individual might be.

That's correct.

When it comes right down to it, I could never realize all of these ideas as an individual contributor. In addition, no matter how wide my circle of influence might be, I can't oversee the progression of all of these ideas either. I've chosen to be a builder; that takes up most of my time.

I'm pleased, however, that I have so many great ideas to pursue. Is there a way for the company to roll forward some of the ideas I've generated?

This brings me to the last section of the book. What if there existed a company that targeted people that were full of ideas?

People who live for innovation.

What if this company designed systems and processes to pull people (like me) out of the trenches (temporarily!) to talk about their plans and dreams?

What if this company funded the best ideas that were discovered as part of this process?

And what if this company actually recognized these innovators and called them the lifeblood of the technology industry?

What would you call such a company?

I'd call it "the company you keep."

15. The Company You Keep

In the spring of 2007, the chief technology officer of EMC, Jeff Nick, announced that EMC was building a "new and improved innovative culture."

I rolled my eyes.

Jeff arrived at EMC after a long career at IBM, where he had been selected as an IBM Fellow.

My assumption was that Jeff would borrow from his IBM background and begin staffing dedicated research facilities around the world with the best and brightest thinkers that money could buy. Members of these teams would receive free lab coats, pocket protectors, and calculators. I was fairly certain that our new CTO would head in that direction.

I was wrong.

Instead, EMC's CTO rolled out a proposal that really, really caught my attention. He announced a call for ideas.

Innovation by contest.

EMC is not the first company to run a contest. However, I sensed something different about this particular call for ideas.

It was targeted at the employees working in the trenches.

Any employee from anywhere in the world could submit an idea. From this level playing field, thirty ideas would be selected. Each idea would be presented, in person, to corporate executives. Marketing employees would work with each inventor to generate a poster of their idea. It would be a global science fair.

News of this contest reached me as I sat at my desk reading my e-mail. My executive visibility at this point was virtually zero. I had recently been transferred to a new organization that was building an innovative new product (product A) from scratch. These types of groups are under a lot of pressure at EMC (i.e., pressure to ship a product and start generating revenue). I was heavily into get-it-done mode and usually didn't participate in corporate initiatives such as this.

The more I thought about submitting an idea, however, the more I liked it. I actually started feeling excited (which isn't my usual response to a corporate e-mail).

I called up my co-worker and fellow blue sky innovator, the CTO of the grid business unit. He and I hadn't spoken much since our collaboration on the Centera data lineage idea. I asked him if he had heard about the contest and whether he had thought about entering. We both felt strongly that the idea was a good one, so we submitted it. Our idea joined over four hundred others from around the globe.

In August 2007, our idea was accepted as one of the thirty finalists. We worked with a marketing employee to create a poster. On the day of the innovation conference, he had to travel. It would be up to me to present our poster to the executives.

In October 2007, at EMC's first Innovation Showcase, our idea was awarded second place.

At the time, I was shocked. Looking back now, I shouldn't have been. Data lineage is a real customer problem, and we had generated a fairly simple solution by combining adjacent technologies. The executives recognized this, and gave us high marks in their grading.

In November 2007, I received another surprise. EMC began to productize the idea. I was assigned to serve as a consultant to a team of software engineers in our R&D facility in Shanghai, China. I was flabbergasted. Why?

Because I had never seen companies reward the people working in the trenches in this way.

Jeff Nick and his team didn't know me from a hole in the wall. But they did know that we had generated a really,

really good idea. So they gave us a reward. They funded us. Out of the blue (or the blue sky). I thought this was really cool. Then it got better.

Six months later, we showed the idea to customers. For the first time, EMC customers saw a solution to a very real problem they experienced every day. How did these customers respond?

They handed out their business cards and said, "Keep me posted on this one.".

My skepticism for this new and improved innovative culture has disappeared completely.

I have learned more about the motivation for creating this new culture and the reason behind creating an annual Innovation Showcase. I like to call this reason "innovative unity." As an organization, EMC is a melting pot of acquired companies and technologies. It had operated as a collection of stovepipes; we all knew there were other stovepipes beyond our own, but we didn't know what they did. Because each stovepipe had, prior to acquisition, operated independently, there were a lot of disparate technology strategies. And most of all, there was a lack of communication across all of the technologies.

Unity was required.

The decision was made to create a yearly focal point to pull all of these organizations together: The Innovation Showcase was born.

Once per year is not enough, however. There are more elements to the new culture.

During the Innovation Conference, an EMC vice president named Chuck Hollis stood up to speak about the importance of employee unity via social media software. Chuck implored all employees to begin blogging and collaborating on EMC ONE, the company's social media site. Chuck was announcing this tool to enable collaboration among all employees (not just the innovators).

I am a person who is drawn to new ideas and opportunities. I was strongly influenced by both the Innovation Showcase and the invitation to participate in EMC ONE. In fact, I decided to join the Innovation Showcase planning team. I also started writing and blogging on EMC ONE. For practice, I created a series of blogs that detailed every idea and product I had launched over my entire career.

Something interesting happened. I began building relationships with people from all around the world. I didn't know any of them. Inevitably, I would write something that would trigger them to respond. These people were in the trenches. They were building, selling, supporting, or marketing EMC's products. Many of them had incredible customer insight.

Suddenly, all of the ingredients for my own personal brand of innovation were at my fingertips.

I was still the expert in my own domain of expertise.

I was reading commentary about customer problems written by employees working directly in the trenches with our customers.

I was collaborating with experts in adjacent spheres throughout the corporation.

During my career, innovation had been a monthly thing, at best. Spurts of innovation would occur over the course of a few weeks or months, and then product development would occur over the course of many months or even years.

I found that EMC's culture empowered me to innovate on a daily basis. Constant exposure to adjacent spheres and customer problems were the fuel for new ideas to put on the back burner and move back burner ideas up to the daily innovation column and beyond.

Interestingly enough, I was drawn to problems that had nothing to do with building products. I dove into these problems part-time as a back burner activity. For example:

- When I joined the Innovation Conference planning committee, the other committee members were looking for new ideas on how to plan next year's conference. I suggested tapping into a global advisory board via EMC ONE.

- I learned that EMC's customers didn't have much visibility into how their products were being built. I decided to start my own external blog and gave it the tagline, "Building Software for the Storage Industry."

- I discovered that my co-workers in human resources were attempting to communicate a common, united employee message across the internal employee base. I also learned that this message was being communicated externally as part of EMC's employment brand. I began my own series of internal and external posts that highlighted aspects of life at EMC.

- The internal employee talk radio show, VTR, was forming. I suggested turning it into a visual talk radio show by creating an Internet video feed showing personal and corporate photographs of guests during the live show.

The generation of these and other ideas became a daily, common occurrence for me. Suddenly my large company (over 35,000 employees) felt a lot smaller. I began to meet and collaborate with expert co-workers around the globe. I would have globally visible, electronic discussions with them about new ideas. I began to learn more about my company.

And my company began to learn more about me. As a result of my involvement with the Innovation Showcase and EMC ONE platform, my visibility grew. My passion for innovation and creativity had found a corporate outlet, and people noticed.

In October 2008 I was recognized as a Distinguished Engineer at EMC. This is a very, very hard honor to achieve. I participated in the Innovation Contest again, and entered my Centera VMware digital archiving idea from the JFK Library. There were 984 world-wide entries in 2008. I came in second.

I was honored at the EMC Distinguished Engineer and Fellow Gala for my patent work. As I shook EMC Chief Executive Officer Joe Tucci's hand that night, he said "You're a real overachiever, aren't you? I appreciate it."

My external blog, called the Information Playground, has turned into a strong customer source for information about how EMC's products are being built. Most of the customers arrive at my blog via google. They are typically searching for information about CLARiiON, or Centera, or PowerPath. I've written about all of these topics. As a result of my blog, I've become recognized in the storage industry for the first time.

I've joined with EMC's PR team to do joint press releases.

My blog is referenced by human resources to help recruit potential employees wishing to learn about EMC's culture.

I've set the record straight on incorrect statements made about my company's products.

I'm not the only person who's received more visibility. The true innovative leaders within EMC are all bubbling to the surface. Geographic distance is no longer an obstacle. The company has become more unified; experts collaborate together internally and externally.

These experts collaborate with employees working in the trenches worldwide. There are no centralized ivory towers of innovation. It's a globally distributed network of ideas coming directly from the people who interact with customers.

In the spring of 2007, EMC's chief technology officer, Jeff Nick, announced that EMC was building a new and improved innovative culture.

And they did.

16. Potential Energy

I have served as a caretaker of the world's information for a long, long time. I do believe that the culture at my corporation will continue to generate innovative new products that satisfy the world's information needs.

I know this because I can see the potential energy.

Potential energy is defined this way on Wikipedia: "Energy stored within a physical system that has the potential to be converted into other forms of energy."

I would like to take the liberty of coining a new term that applies to the innovative capacity of large corporate organizations: *corporate potential energy*. Here's how I define corporate potential energy: "product innovation stored within corporate employees that has the potential to be converted into other forms of product innovation."

I can think of no better way to illustrate corporate potential energy than figure 41. The figure is filled with a partial list of EMC's large number of products; the whole list wouldn't fit on one page, let alone in one little diagram. This diagram represents a subset of EMC's adjacent technologies, and I have drawn lines between the technologies that I have been personally involved with or otherwise described within the pages of this book.

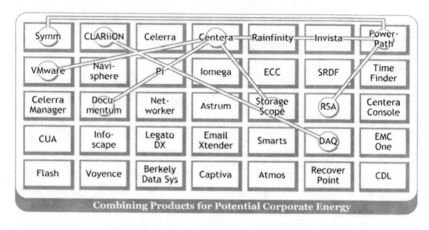

Figure 41. Potential corporate energy is based on combining products.

The connections in figure 41 represent adjacent technologies. Most of these technologies are related to information storage because that is my background.

Consider, for example, my background with the Centera product. I can use figure 41 as an innovation dartboard. Imagine I throw a dart and it hits InfoScape. I don't know a lot about that product, but I do know it's involved with the discovery, search, and indexing of information. Perhaps InfoScape could discover, search, and index the content on a Centera?

Or I could throw a dart and hit Captiva. Captiva takes distributed business-critical information such as paper, faxes, and electronic content and allows enterprises to process and organize these items. I wonder what customer problems could be addressed by combining these two products?

At some point in time, I am likely to tire of re-architecting my current product and will decide to leave. I likely wouldn't leave the company! I would chase the next light bulb, transfer to an adjacent technology, spend six months attempting to become an expert, and then begin a new innovative process.

I could transfer to a new group every year until I retire, and I wouldn't be able to visit them all. That's variety. That makes me want to stay.

Everyone who works at EMC is in the same boat, although many of them don't know it (at least not yet). EMC now has an internal innovation roadmap for every employee. That roadmap looks like this:

1. Become an expert in your technology. Get it done.
2. Take a leadership role. Lead from the trenches.
3. Participate in the internal Innovation Network on EMC ONE.
   a. Identify customer problems.
   b. Identify adjacent technologies.
4. Propose an idea.
   a. Submit it to EMC ONE.
   b. Submit it to the Innovation Conference.
   c. Use your influence as appropriate.
5. Be persistent.

I am fairly certain I will walk this path several more times in my career. Whatever project I am working on will be completed, and I will face a choice: do I re-architect, or do I leave?

If I choose to leave, I have found (over and over again) that, by choosing to stay within my company, I have maintained a level of influence that has allowed my ideas to eventually be consumed by customers! I do not want to innovate for the sake of innovation. I want to innovate to have a positive and significant impact on the world's use of information.

I wrote this book with innovative employees in mind. I've argued that the potential for innovation is greatest at large companies with the right innovative culture. By large companies, I am implying a corporation with many adjacent technologies that all focus on or close to a targeted customer problem. My company, for example, is trying to solve only one problem: taking care of customer information.

I hope that I've reached my target audience and given creative employees a blueprint for personal innovation.

I imagine there are customers who will someday read this book as well. To them I say, "Thank you." Keep those cards and problems coming. I'm working on some new ideas.

My company now ships a product that is small enough to sit on top of your desk, right next to your computer. It's called Iomega.

We also ship a product that is big enough to span continents. It's called Atmos.

I'd like to work on a galactic storage system.

The next phase of my career will see a sharp increase in the direct collaboration between multiple customers and the innovators creating their products. This collaboration should be public and is long overdue. You own your sphere, I'll own mine, and we'll jointly find an adjacent sphere.

You can trust me, and my company, with your information.

We'll take care of it.

About The Author

Steve Todd is a husband of more than twenty years, a father to two children, and, except for his college years, a lifelong Massachusetts resident. His focus on his family and community is the driving force behind all that he does. An avid athlete, coach, counselor, playwright/director, musician, and mentor, Steve spent several summers raising his children in the bleachers of Fenway Park, and then took them out of school for a six-week cross-country camping trip from one coast of America to the other and back again.

Steve was formally trained in software engineering at the University of New Hampshire, from which he earned both bachelor's and master's degrees in computer science. He is a dues-paying member of Mensa International and, throughout his career, has focused his brainpower on creating better, faster, more useful information storage technology. A strong collaborator, his innovative ideas have yielded products that are used by consumers, governments, and museums throughout the world, as well as 150 patent applications and billions of dollars in revenue for his corporation.

Steve promotes his personal style of innovation with employees, students, and corporations alike and, as a result of his lifelong contribution to the information technology industry, was recently named a Distinguished Engineer for EMC Corporation, one of the largest providers of information and storage technology in the world. He publishes a technology blog known as the *Information Playground.*

LaVergne, TN USA
07 September 2010
196036LV00001B/2/P